High Intensity Guitar Technique Book 2

PROFESSIONAL TECHNIQUES

Anthony George

All of the bonus audio and video files included with this book can be accessed for free at
www.cuttingedge.guitars/higt2bonus

First published in Great Britain in 2019

For advanced online guitar courses, lesson packs and more, visit Anthony George's all-in-one online learning platform - Cutting Edge Guitar at the address below.

www.cuttingedge.guitars

High Intensity Guitar Technique Book 2/ Anthony George. —1st ed.
ISBN 9781086384765

Contents

Foreword 1

Introduction 3

Legato 6

Alternate Picking 22

Sweep Picking 35

Tapping 45

Developing Speed 54

Advanced String Bending and Vibrato 63

Licks and Musical Phrases 74

Continued Development 93

    Sample five hour technique practice routine 100

Jam Tracks 108

Afterword 115

This book is dedicated to all students of the guitar, and all of the amazing musicians who inspired me to want to write it. Mainly this book is dedicated to Lavinia, for her continued belief, strength and support.

Foreword

The **High Intensity Guitar Technique** book series has been designed to equip modern guitar players with the techniques required to play any music style they desire. This second book of this series is aimed at intermediate to advanced guitarists looking to expand their technical skill, in order to be able to play more intricate music. The examples in this book have been written in a combination of standard music notation and tablature. There are also some fretboard diagrams that map out the important scales we need in order to play the exercises.

All of the bonus audio and video files that support the book can be downloaded for free from **www.cuttingedge.guitars/higt2bonus** . There are also seven backing tracks included with the audio so that you can practise jamming using your newfound technical ability. There is a chapter at the end of the book that explains the best way to play over the tracks.

When I look back to the 14-year-old me, sat on my bed listening to Yngwie Malmsteen and Joe Satriani, all I wanted to do was be able to play guitar in a similar fashion. The problem was that I had only one simple scale shape, and just tried to play up and down it as fast as humanly possible. I ached for a document that had all of the answers, one book that would show me what these guys were doing. It is my sincerest hope that in the **High Intensity Guitar Technique** series is that answer.

This book will give you a comprehensive guitar workout, which will keep your technical skills at an exceptionally high level and in the process open up your mind to many possibilities that you perhaps would not have come up with on your own. In short, this book will help you to be a better guitar player. Please remember that the music you are trying to play is always the most important and the most fundamental issue; the techniques should not be the driving force of your music, but merely the vehicle that allows it to flow.

The ideas and techniques presented in this series are the culmination of ten years worth of incessant practice, research, trial and error on my part. Every single technique and exercise I present here has been used by myself to satisfy a need in my own playing and has been tested on hundreds of guitarists throughout my career as a teacher.

All of these exercises have worked for me, or an individual I have taught, but not everything works for everyone. When using these books please let them also help you to find your own unique style and your own 'voice' on the guitar. You do not have to master everything here, but please do at least give it a good go before deciding you don't like it, or that it doesn't fit with your own playing.

It takes time and effort to become a technically accomplished guitar player; it doesn't come easy to anyone. We all must work hard, but if you truly love playing the guitar and making music with this wonderful instrument, it won't feel like work at all. You will just enjoy it.

Some of my favourite times as a guitar player were in those teenage years when I couldn't play anything other than that one scale. Purely because the progression element was so exciting, witnessing myself improving every day and getting more excited about the new things I was going to learn. This is the stage that you are now in, having picked up this book, and I'm so glad to be accompanying you on your journey.

Have fun.

Introduction

Welcome to Book Two of the **High Intensity Guitar Technique** series. In Book One of this series we looked at the foundations of guitar playing technique, and building a solid grasp of the basic mechanics of modern guitar playing. Mastering these basic mechanics allows us to play efficiently, so we can sound as musical as possible when playing, writing and improvising. Book Two will follow on from Book One and take you to a professional level of technique for legato, alternate picking, sweep picking, tapping and also a more advanced approach to string bending and vibrato.

In Book Two we will explore how to expand on the technique areas that we covered in Book One by looking at more complex examples. These will include more demanding cyclic exercises, which will form the building blocks for real guitar licks, more complex and intricate runs, sequences and of course, building our speed to play faster and more technical music. Later in the book, you will find chapter 7 is dedicated purely to licks that you can use in your own improvised solos or of course your own compositions.

Although these are very musical ideas they may not directly have a place in your music or your own playing, but you can certainly use the licks as a springboard to create your own music. The main goal of this book is to take your technique up to the next level and make your playing sound more polished and professional.

Many of the examples will be pentatonic (five note scale) based as this is a 'standard' or 'go to' scale for the lead guitar player. Many guitarists tend to snub pentatonic playing as 'basic' playing. You will find that there is nothing basic about the examples here, they are challenging, even for advanced players. Also remember that when anything is 'standard' on the guitar, it is usually because it sounds good, and as the old adage goes 'if it sounds good, it is good'.

We will also be looking at the foundations of three notes per string playing in this book. Three notes per string playing is exactly what it says on the tin. You play through scales, using three notes, on every string. This kind of playing is more commonly associated with the major scale and its modes. We will discuss this later in the book when we look at the relevant techniques that require three notes per string playing. We will also cover some more advanced arpeggio concepts in this book, so we are covering a lot of ground.

The book will be broken down into nine chapters, one for each technique covered, a chapter dedicated purely to building speed and a chapter dedicated to licks. There is a chapter dedicated to continued development, showing you what to do once you've finished the book, and finally a chapter to support the jam tracks on the accompanying downloads for the book. I have included the jam tracks to give you a way to practise playing with your newfound techniques.

The chapters are ordered:

1. Legato.
2. Alternate Picking.
3. Sweep Picking.
4. Tapping.
5. Developing Speed.
6. Advanced String Bending and Vibrato.
7. Licks and Musical Phrases.
8. Continued Development.
9. Jam Tracks.

You will find the chapters are ordered in quite a methodical manner, as each chapter prepares you for the next. The legato chapter will sufficiently prepare the fretting hand to be able to cope with what it needs to do for the picking sections. Once you've worked on syncing the two hands with your picking sections it will be easier to work on the tapping examples.

The developing speed chapter comes after all of the exercises for the four chief areas of guitar technique. You will need to have a solid foundation in how to perform all of the exercises before you try and push through the speed barrier. I've put the string bending examples after these chapters, as string bending is usually used as a way to exit licks, such as the ones we will cover. You can use your current bending ideas from Book One to exit the licks and examples throughout the book. In the advanced string bending chapter, I just want to give you some new ideas and directions to go in with the technique.

I think it's also a good place to put this technique just before the licks chapter. I thoroughly recommend working through the book in a methodical manner, and as there is plenty of string bending happening in the licks chapter, it makes sense to have worked on the technique to a seriously in-depth level before attempting the licks.

I recommend working on all of the examples in the book in a progressive way, for you to gain as much from the examples as possible. Once you've spent many hours working on all of the examples in this book you will find that your technique has really gone to the next level. Once you've been through the book methodically you can then dip back in at particular points you feel need work. You must also make sure to be practising the ideas in as many different keys and within your own musical styles as soon as possible. This will make the ideas presented as useable to you as they can be.

Throughout the book I will give details on how best to practise each exercise in order to get the most from it. So make sure you're playing the examples in the right way to get the best out of them. As with Book One, make sure you have each lick completely under your fingers before applying speed. Always remember the best way to play something fast is to master it slowly.

As with Book One, all of the examples from Book Two are available as a free audio download from my website **www.cuttingedge.guitars/higt2bonus** On the download I have demonstrated each example slowly, so you can fully hear how each example should be played, and then I have demonstrated it 'up to tempo' so you can hear how the example sounds at a more musical speed.

Play each lick at a 'learn' speed for about a week before trying to apply speed. A learn speed of around 60 bpm usually works for most students on sixteenth notes or sextuplet rhythm values. Make sure though to play at whatever speed is comfortable for you to get yourself started. Any of the techniques outlined in Book One for playing these ideas up to tempo will work brilliantly for you, so I highly recommend employing those techniques with these exercises. There is no better way though than starting slowly, and gradually increasing your metronome or drum machine in small increments over periods of time.

Listen to your own hands, they will tell you what they are technically capable of achieving. Remember speed is a by-product of accuracy, and it takes time to build. Also don't forget that not only metronomes and drum machines are good for playing along to, but also backing tracks that you can slow down with software such as Amazing Slow Downer or Transcribe!. Practising this way gives you the feeling of playing along with real music. Once again, gradually increase the speed over periods of time.

OK, guitar players, let's get stuck in.

CHAPTER 1

Legato

As we discovered in Book One, legato is an Italian word that translates as 'tied together'. What it means in musical terms is that you need to play a phrase smoothly. To us as guitar players that means we need to play everything with hammer-ons, pull-offs and slides. You will notice as a guitarist that when you use your pick for everything it has an aggressive attack in tone, but when you play with hammer-ons and pull-offs you can get a really smooth and bubbly effect.

Most guitar players tend to find that they can play legato passages far faster than they can play picked lines. The reason is that when you are playing legato lines you only really need to be thinking about what you're doing in the fretting hand, and not worrying about getting the synchronization between both hands on the guitar.

As a young guitarist I always favoured the legato approach as it felt more natural and easier to play fast, and it was only when I realized the tonal difference I was missing out on that I really got stuck in to sorting out my alternate picking chops. Due to the legato technique having this wonderful smooth tone and it being easier to play more things up to speed this way, you will actually find that the legato approach is the most dominant technique in lead guitar playing.

Absolutely every player from every genre has to be familiar with the legato technique in order to have a rounded approach to the guitar. Players as diverse as B.B. King, Brad Paisley and Steve Vai all have an excellent facility for using legato, yet they all play completely different styles. The first exercises and licks we will look at in this chapter about the legato technique are all centred on advanced pentatonic concepts. We will be looking at runs and sequences that span the width and the length of the neck, to show you how you can use this technique to break out of common 'box' playing and have a lot more freedom on the neck. Later in the chapter we will introduce three notes per string legato based on major scale concepts.

Legato can be used for all kinds of guitar playing but it certainly lends itself well to pentatonic style licks, as with the two notes per string set-up of the scale it's actually quite demanding to alternate pick. Before getting stuck in to the exercises, it would be well worth spending a decent amount of time using some of the warming up ideas we looked at in Book One to prevent yourself getting some nasty injuries. For those of you unfamiliar with Book One of this series it would be very good for you to use some warm-up exercises before steaming in to this section, not only to prevent injury but it will also make the exercises much easier to perform.

Also, it would be well worth recapping the five minor pentatonic shapes from Book One as some of these ideas can be played in more than one position. I would strongly urge you to see if it's possible to perform these ideas in as many positions and as always in as many keys as possible, thus making them totally useable on the whole fretboard. It could actually serve as a pretty decent warm-up just spending ten to twenty minutes at the beginning of your practice routine playing up and down the five pentatonic positions. Once you're familiar with the scale and are nicely warmed up, it's time to take a look at Example 1.

Example 1 is an extremely common ascending run for the minor pentatonic scale. I've written it in sixteenth note triplets (six notes per click) but it can be written in triplets (three notes per click). It was first used by players such as Jimmy Page, and was one of the signature types of lick that put him on the map. It was then of course copied and used by all sorts of players such as Randy Rhoads and Eddie Van Halen and pretty much any rock guitarist that has followed.

Blues players such as Stevie Ray Vaughan have used this sort of thing, at speed, for their signature sounds. It's kind of a pentatonic speed lick, but also if slowed down and played with swing feel gives a nice bluesy effect. I recommend using fingers 1 and 4 to start off with, 1 and 3 for the middle strings and then your personal preference of either 1 and 4 or 1 and 3 for the top two strings. All approaches are valid, it's a case of finding what works for you.

Example 1

Example 2 is a straight sixteenth note idea in the style of Paul Gilbert. Paul is a stunning rock guitar player who always manages to find the coolest ways of phrasing pentatonic licks. This particular sequence is based on position one, and is quite tricky to finger, but has an awesome rock guitar appeal. I've exited the lick with a full tone bend and wide vibrato to demonstrate how it is used in rock applications. Use fingers 1 and 4 to start and then whatever feels comfortable from then on. Make sure the lick is completely under your fingers before trying to apply speed.

Example 2

Example 3 is another Paul Gilbert style sequencing idea that will span the whole of position one A minor pentatonic. It's a one bar sequence that we play on different string groupings until we reach the top of the scale. Once at the top of the scale we perform a tone bend rock style exit. I would recommend that you practise the one bar sequence for a while before trying to move it around the rest of the scale. Are there any other pentatonic shapes that the ideas so far looked at would work in? Try it out and see. If not, can you adapt a lick to make your own for a different position? This way you will start developing your own unique style.

Example 3

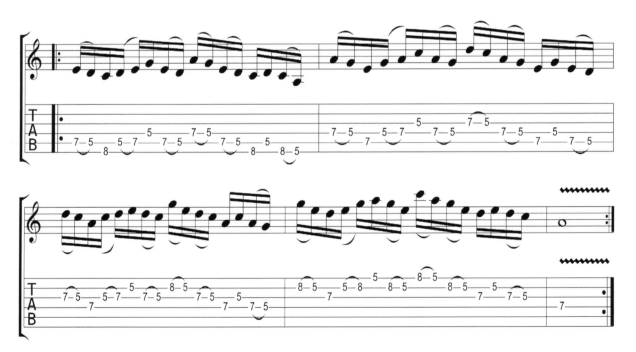

Example 4 is a descending run that is often found in the playing of guitarists such as Eric Johnson, Joe Bonamassa, Joe Satriani and Shawn Lane. This sort of idea can be picked or played legato, but has a really smooth and bubbly quality about it when played legato. I would keep the pick moving in the same direction as the strings with this one to get the smoothest sound possible. Once again, see if you can make this idea work in other pentatonic positions. You can get some quite monstrous licks when combining different shapes with this approach. Take a listen to the solo from 'When the Sun Meets the Sky' by Eric Johnson, or 'Rubina' by Joe Satriani to hear this used to great effect.

Example 4

Example 5 is a bit of a collaboration of several sequences in one lick. It has a really good effect on the listener as it is less predictable than just doing one sequence through an entire shape. First we have a descending version of a twelve note sequence being played over two beats, then we have a six note sequence which is played for two beats, then in the second bar we have the Eric Johnson style run we just looked at being played descending, then ascending. There's quite a bit to get to grips with in this lick, but trust me, it's worth it. The lick sounds very impressive at speed.

Example 5

The next example is very much inspired by guitar legend Shawn Lane. Shawn is well known for being one of the most preposterously fast guitar players of all time, yet also had such an immense sense of melody, phrasing and an innate sense of musicality. It's little wonder that he has inspired techniques throughout this series.

This example is based on a new type of rhythmic feel called quintuplets. This means we will be playing five notes per beat, which is very odd in western music. We do not hear this kind of rhythmic grouping very often; it does, however, produce great sounds when playing really fast licks, and often makes more sense when performed at speed rather than slowly. The lick involves lots of the rolling technique discussed in Book One, and is our first lick that will use multiple positions of the pentatonic scale, starting in position five and ending in position two.

Be careful that you are fingering it in a sensible fashion. I personally favour a 2-1-3-1-3 fingering to start and then use fingers 1 and 3 wherever possible throughout the rest of the lick. It may be worth looping just one beat to a metronome in order to get the feel of playing quintuplets in time. It may also help you to say a word with five syllables to the click in order to get the feel for timing. For example, words like hippopotamus or telemarketing have five syllables, so try saying them to a click to get the feel.

Example 6

At the end of Example 6 there was a slight position shift from position five to position one and then two. In Example 7 we will be traversing the neck much more, starting in position five then very quickly going into position one and then two again to finish. Licks in this way give you much more freedom of the neck and allow you to play much longer and more flowing lines. This sort of idea is not genre specific; all the greatest guitarists from all genres use these kinds of ideas.

Example 7

Example 8 shows a run that moves in and out of positions going along just a pair of strings. A common approach for traversing the neck with any scale type is playing patterns on two strings and moving it along the neck.

Example 8

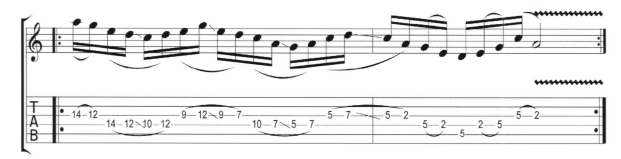

Example 9 shows a more elaborate way of using more than one shape. We start by playing a sequenced idea through shape one A minor pentatonic, then moving into position two and then three, before playing a different type of sequence to finish the lick, staying in position three. This sort of idea can be used to give you some nice extended runs and break you out of standard positional playing ruts.

You may find that using the strict fingerings we have used when playing up and down the scale shapes don't fit very well with the run in this example. Get creative and find the fingering that works best for you. As always, take it slow at first and make sure you aren't piling on the speed before you're able to play the whole run accurately. You can also play small bite-sized parts of the run on their own until you build up to the whole lick.

Example 9

Example 10 is a fast-paced rock or fusion style lick that is played in all five positions along the top two strings. Once you have the initial basic pattern down you are just playing it in all five pentatonic positions along the neck. This is a common approach for many guitar styles and can be found in the playing of rock guitarists like Andy Timmons and Richie Kotzen, but can equally be found in the playing of blues giants such as Joe Bonamassa and once again fusion aficionado Shawn Lane used this sort of idea.

Example 10

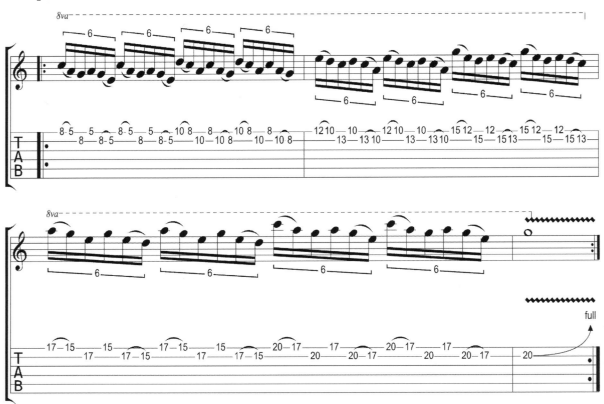

The next of our legato examples for this chapter is a very challenging example in the style, once again, of Eric Johnson. Eric is well known across the globe for his wonderful guitar playing. His phrasing, timing, sense of feel, his knowledge of harmony and an extreme sense of musicality make him a truly wonderful guitarist. He is very fond of using a cascading effect and often uses sextuplets and quintuplets to get his super fast approach. He often links pentatonic shapes together in a three notes per string fashion, and that's exactly how we start our example. You will be combining notes from position four of the Am pentatonic scale and position five.

Set up your fingers so you have a 4-3-1 fingering on the first three notes of this example. From there on in you want to be using fingers 1 and 3 all the way with this example. Watch out for the nasty position shift halfway through beat three in which you will quickly need to slide the first finger from the fourth position into the third position. From there it's just a standard descending run, but achieving the speed that Eric gets will certainly cause problems. Check out his album *Venus Isle* for loads of this style of playing.

Example 11

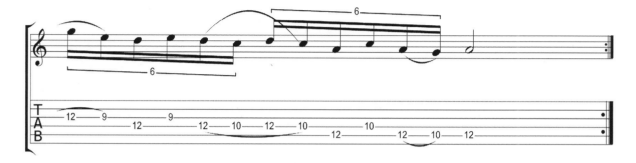

That should be enough pentatonic ideas to keep you busy for quite some time. Once you have these ideas sorted as I've written them, try coming up with fresh ways to play them by using these ideas in different positions of the pentatonic scale. Get creative and come up with your own licks that you can use in your playing, to develop your own unique style.

At this point we need to introduce the three notes per string system for further enhancement of our legato technique. I'm sure many of you reading this book have heard the term 'three notes per string', as it's a term commonly associated with high level guitar playing. You perhaps aren't sure of the exact meaning of this term, so we need to clear this up before we start learning any shapes.

Essentially any scale can be played on the guitar in a three notes per string fashion. What this means, is that you will play three notes of a scale on one string, then move to the next string, and then play the next three notes of that scale. Guitar players like these three notes per string shapes as they fit very nicely under the fingers of the fretting hand, and they also lend themselves to faster ways to play the guitar.

Although we can play any scale in three notes per string form, when we refer to three notes per string playing, we are usually talking about the major scale or modes of the major scale concepts. The three notes per string variations of the major scale are the most common approach for most technical work by modern rock and fusion guitarists.

The nature of the scale forms allows faster passages to be more easily executed, and is much easier to create longer flowing lines than the box positions. It is worth noting that there are seven three notes per string shapes on the neck rather than the usual five CAGED shapes. This is because there is a shape built on each degree of the major scale, which is a seven note scale.

Figure 1 and Figure 2 are diagrams that show all seven positions of the three notes per string forms for the C major scale. I've first written them in numerical position order in Figure 1, then I've written them in the order that they play across the neck in Figure 2, from the lowest to highest position. You will need to spend plenty of time learning those shapes before you can start looking at the legato exercises I have written for them. These examples will be based around small sections of the shapes of which you can (and should) be moving to different shapes around the neck to be able to utilize the technique fully, so it is absolutely essential that you know the shapes inside out.

To do so you can employ any of your favourite arpeggiator techniques from Book One. Your best bet at first will be to play each individual shape in every position along the neck. For example, you could take the first position of the major scale and play it up and down in the first fret area of the neck. Then you could move to the second fret position and repeat. This will not only enable you to learn each shape and get plenty of mileage from practising up and down it, but also hear it in all twelve keys, thus training your ear.

Once you have each individual shape under your fingers, you should play up and down them as they play out across the neck, in key, and as they are written on the scale diagrams. Finally, you should play up one, down two, up three, down four etc. until you have completed the whole neck. That way all seven shapes should be nicely bedded in. Playing through the shapes in this fashion gives you the ability to freely move between the shapes.

With the freedom you will garner from moving between the shapes, it makes it a lot easier for you to creatively improvise, or learn the solos of your favourite players that utilize this type of playing. I have written a tab example of how to perform this exercise after the scale diagrams, aptly called linking the three notes per string shapes.

FIGURE 1

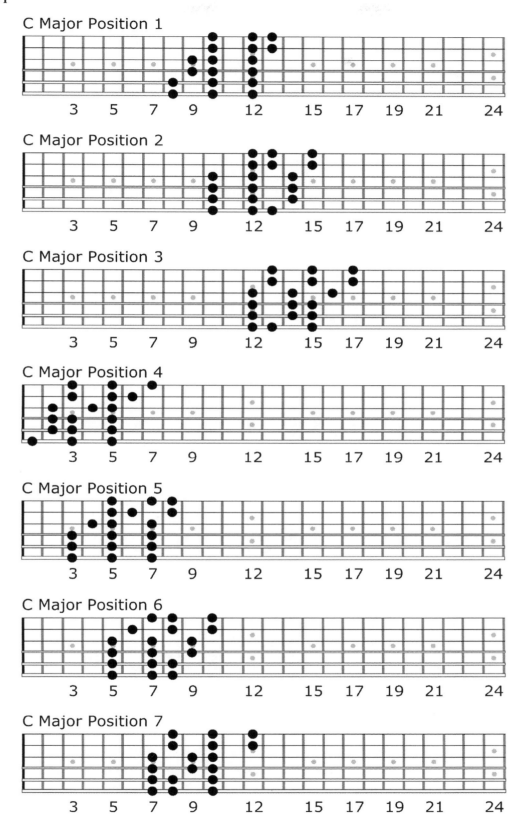

FIGURE 2

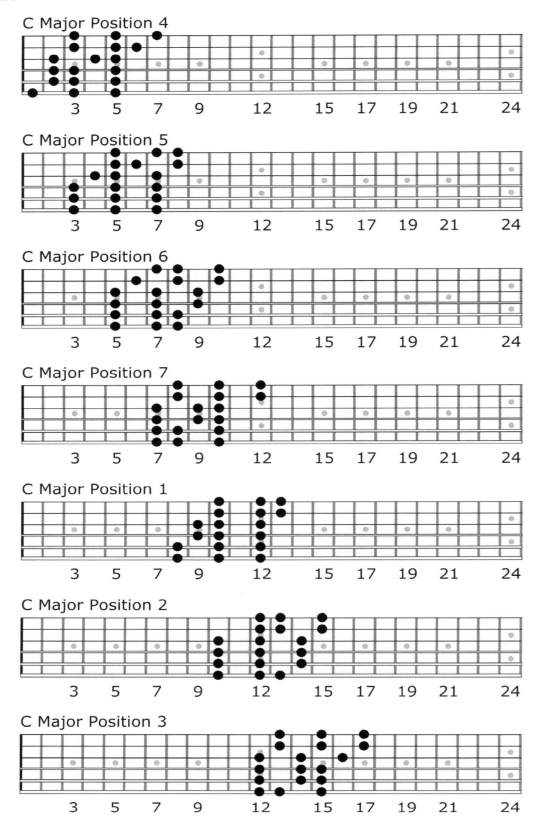

As I mentioned earlier, I will now outline in tab how to correctly link up the seven major scale shapes. I've written the exercise moving from the lowest position of the scale (position four) through to the high C at the twentieth fret on the high E string. When performing this exercise use your preferred type of technique. By all means use alternate or economy picking to learn the shapes. Don't feel they need to be learned using the legato technique, unless of course you want to do it that way.

Linking the three notes per string shapes

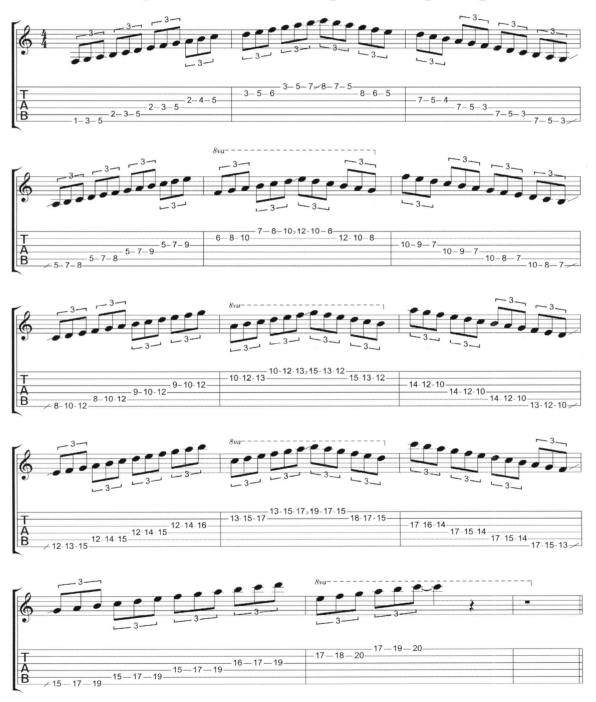

Once you have the three notes per string shapes sufficiently bedded in, you are ready to begin looking at Example 12. This is a single cell repetition idea split into two forms, a and b. Example 12a is a forward motion idea on the high E string in position five of our C major scale. You need to use a strict fingering of 1, 3, 4 for this exercise, which is particularly difficult. This is due to the fact that you have to pull-off from the fourth finger, back to the first finger before repeating the lick again. I personally found this particular lick very difficult indeed in the early days of my learning, so take your time. Make sure to play the exercise accurately and slowly to begin with, possibly using triplets to get you started rather than sextuplets at a learn speed of around 60 bpm.

Once you have mastered Example 12a, take a look at 12b. This is the same basic exercise and fingering, yet we have reversed the order of the notes, so that now the lick begins with the fourth finger. You then pull-off down to the third and first finger, before hammering again your fourth, and repeating the lick. Make sure you remember to use all of your correct left and right hand muting techniques from Book One to make sure the lick is executed as cleanly as possible. For example, your first finger should be stubbing up to your second string throughout this lick, and your right hand should be taking care of the lower strings to keep them from ringing.

Example 12a   **12b**

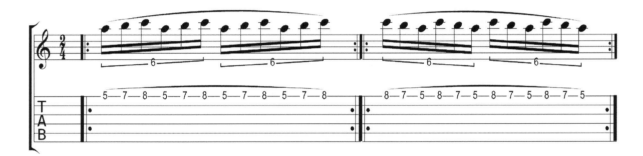

Example 13 shows how you would perform the same idea if you moved it to the next position of the C major scale. This time use a 1, 2, 4 finger combination. All of your muting principles from the previous example are applicable here.

Example 13a   **13b**

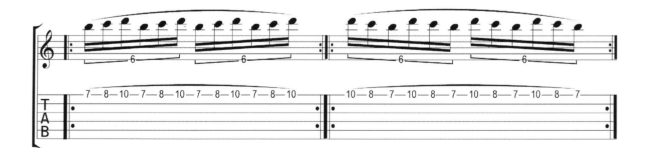

Example 14 shows the third and final fingering for the major scale in three notes per string format. No matter where you are on the neck, if you are playing a major scale (or one of its modes) you will be playing one of the fingerings from Examples 12, 13 and 14. For this example, use again fingers 1, 2 and 4. This time there will be a wider stretch in the hand than before, so be mindful of injuries. Make sure to take rests if you feel any pain.

Example 14a   **14b**

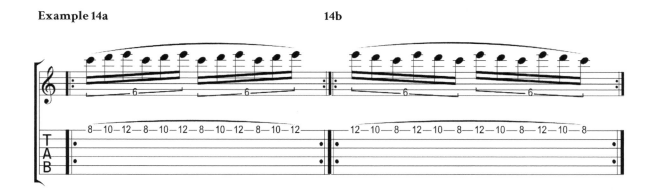

Example 15 shows you the same exercise being played down an octave, so the lick will be found at the fifth fret on the third string. The challenge presented here is the different level of muting you will need to incorporate to make the lick sound clean. Also playing the exercise here will just feel different. I always maintain that you should play these ideas in as many places as possible, and moving things in octaves is quite often a good place to start.

Example 15a   **15b**

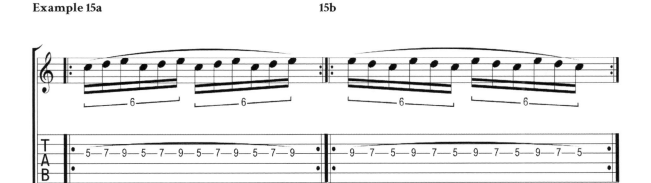

Example 16 shows you how to perform the lick down one more octave. This time it will feel really stretchy in the left hand. The lick is also very difficult to mute when played in this way. Try using fingers from the right hand and the pick, to lie on idle strings to make sure you're playing it as clean and smooth as possible.

Example 16a   **16b**

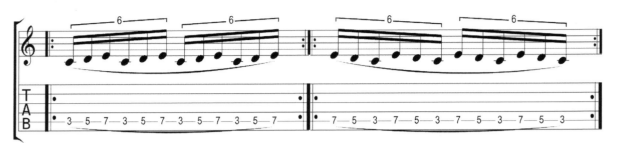

Now that we've spent lots of time looking at how to perform legato ideas on one string, we should start applying some string crossing concepts to three notes per string. When we can cross strings correctly, we can begin linking up the different shapes to create longer, flowing lines that span entire scale shapes. Examples 17a, 17b and 17c show three different fingerings that span the C major scale in position five and six. Remember that when you cross strings you must lead with the first finger to play the new note; in this case it will always be the first finger. Also make sure you are using the correct fingers for the specific exercise.

Example 17a   **17b**   **17c**

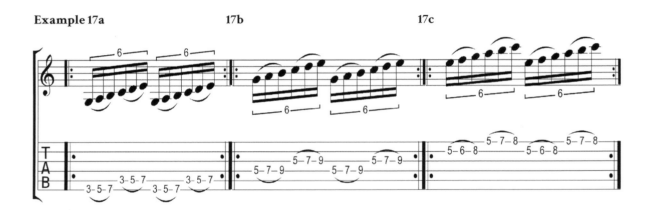

Examples 18a, 18b and 18c show descending versions of this exercise. Emphasizing pull-offs rather than hammer-ons.

Example 18a   **18b**   **18c**

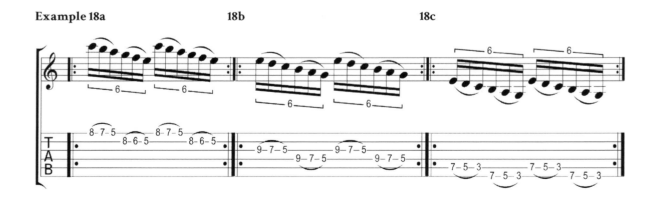

Our final thing to do with these legato exercises is to start combining them. So what you will have next is an exercise that combines the single string approach to half roll legato, and the string crossing idea. In Examples 19a, b and c you will first ascend each string twice, before crossing to the new string. The licks you can create with the following idea are very common in the styles of modern rock and fusion players. Example 19 is an ascending version only of this idea, but once you are confident with it, make sure to play a descending version too.

Example 19a   **19b**   **19c**

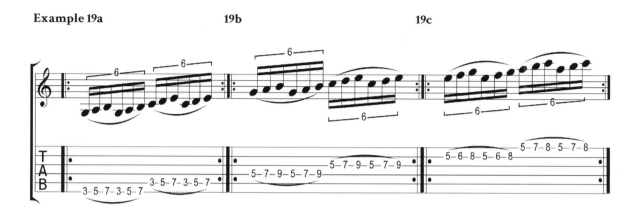

In this chapter, we have looked at lots of new ways to expand the legato technique using pentatonic and major/modal scales. Now you need to spend lots of time getting each example under your fingers so that you may use them freely and creatively. Once you have each legato exercise firmly under your fingers, begin working on your speed until you are comfortable at playing these kinds of ideas at musical tempos. Start trying to incorporate your newfound technique into your own licks and improvisation to start getting the best out of them.

To find out more about how to incorporate this technique into your playing, I would recommend listening to and transcribing the music of Joe Satriani. He is a player who is very fond of this technique and plays this way on lots of his albums. Once you have a good facility for the legato exercises we have covered, head on over to the alternate picking chapter for a new direction in your playing.

CHAPTER 2

Alternate Picking

As the name suggests, alternate picking means that you 'alternate' the direction of stroke you are using every time you play a note. Alternate picking is a strict motion in which we play one note with a downstroke with the plectrum, followed immediately with an upstroke for the next note that we will play. For the rest of the passage you are playing, you continue with down, up, down, up until you have finished playing that particular passage.

In Book One, we looked at the fundamental principles of this technique and started to bed in the strict movement of down followed by up for lines and passages of notes. In this chapter, we are going to build on those foundations, by looking at more demanding string crossing ideas and by playing over all six strings. Also we will be looking at much larger scale passages, which can be used as building blocks for your own runs.

Keep in mind that the way you hold your plectrum has quite an effect on not only the tone you will get from this technique, but also it will be easier to perform the technique if you hold your pick in the correct way. Make sure you are holding the plectrum between the thumb and the first finger of your right hand. Hold the plectrum on the side of your first finger, not on the print part, and have the plectrum sticking out so that the pointed end is angled slightly away from your thumb. If you have the plectrum held correctly this should mean when you bring your picking hand across the guitar's body to pick the strings, the pick should strike the string at roughly a forty-five degree angle. For a detailed view of this, check out the video tutorial included with HIGT Book One.

This angle that you have created will not only allow the pick to easily flow over the strings and give you less resistance when performing these ideas, but will also give you an added bite to your tone. This biting attack adds an aggressive element that guitarists like about alternate picking. If you are a rock player, you may wish to add a little right hand palm muting to your alternate picked licks. This once again adds a little aggression to the tone and also cleans up the muddiness that is created by the attack of the pick.

If you are getting your alternate picked licks right you should be able to hear the pick attacking the strings through your amp. It will make a very rhythmic click sound in addition to the notes you are trying to play. I certainly recommend that you watch some videos of your favourite alternate pickers and try to copy their own unique style. You will find that they all do things slightly differently, but generally the outline I have given you for how to perform alternate picked lines will be a good starting point.

Some notable alternate pickers from the rock genre are Paul Gilbert, who has to my mind probably the best alternate picking technique on the planet, John Petrucci of Dream Theater, Steve Morse and Vinnie Moore to name but a few. For the blues players, once again Eric Johnson has a wonderful facility for this technique, Joe Bonamassa and Gary Moore have fantastic alternate picking capabilities. The jazzers among you may wish to check out John McLaughlin, Al Di Meola and Pat Martino for some wonderful examples of this technique. Lastly the fusion players among you couldn't go wrong with once again Shawn Lane, who interestingly angles his pick backwards, Guthrie Govan and Greg Howe, who all have scary good alternate picking ability.

OK, let's take a look at some examples.

Example 20 picks up where we left off in Book One with our cross string alternate picking. This time we are looking at picking over all six strings, and are using a position one C major arpeggio. You will be playing up and down the arpeggio in triplets, making sure that you are following the strict pick directions written in the example. Make sure you are rolling the third finger correctly on the tenth fret notes and first finger on the top two strings to avoid note bleed. Syncing up the two hands here is quite tricky so take your time.

Example 20

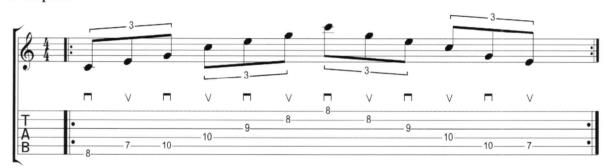

Example 21 is the same thing but with the A minor arpeggio. Once again, watch out for the rolling in the fretting hand to avoid note bleed, and don't try to play the idea faster than you actually can. Use a stopwatch and see if you can play the arpeggios up and down for one minute continuously without making a mistake. If you can, you've pretty much got the idea down. I've not included the pick directions on this example but it should be pretty self-explanatory by now. It is always down followed by up, no exceptions.

Example 21

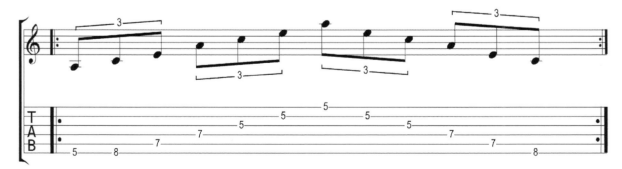

Example 22 shows an alternate fingering for the A minor arpeggio, which presents a different set of pick directions, much the same as we had in our C major example.

Example 22

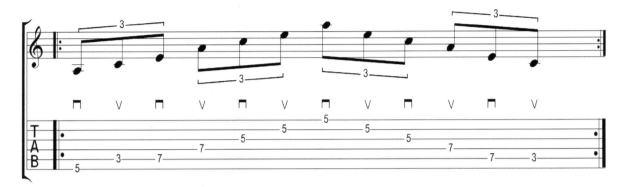

The next example is a large example designed to give you an extended practice etude for the cross string picking idea. What you will be doing is taking the major arpeggio shape, and playing it in three different keys along the neck. Firstly, you will ascend and descend the arpeggio in the key of G at the third fret. Then you will shift it up two frets and play it in the key of A at the fifth fret, before finally shifting up another two frets and playing it ascending and descending in the key of B. Just so you get the maximum out of the idea what you then do, as you may have a guessed, is come back on yourself so that you end up back in the G position. You will end on the G note on the sixth string.

Example 23

To keep Example 23 metronomic, you don't fully descend on the way down, you only come back as far as the major third. This means you can start on the root note of the next arpeggio on beat one of the bar. It's a demanding and long exercise so take your time, and aim to be able to play it with no mistakes from beginning to end. Start slowly but try to build this one up to a reasonable and challenging tempo to get the best results.

This is a tough exercise but it will certainly be giving you lots of mileage on getting your string crossing sorted. If you're able to play the whole thing with no dead notes or mistakes of any kind your alternate picking is now pretty good. There is of course more though, and lots of different ways in which we can stretch this technique to its limit. The first idea I had for making this kind of idea more difficult, was to double up the notes of each arpeggio, and that is what we will encounter in the next example. I took the idea from something I heard in a Dream Theater song, where John Petrucci is playing an arpeggio sequence where he doubles up all of the notes.

For our example we are keeping the three unrelated major arpeggios and playing up and down each one in turn but playing each note of the arpeggio twice. This means we have swapped from a triplet feel to a sixteenth note feel. We are, however, keeping our idea of descending each arpeggio only as far as the major third before moving on to the next arpeggio. We are also only playing this exercise forwards, and not coming back, as it's very tricky. So your last note will be the root of the B major arpeggio.

Example 24

The next example takes this idea to its logical conclusion, by adding one more play of each note to the mix. We are now going to go back to a triplet feel and play each note of each arpeggio a full three times before moving to the next note. This will prepare us nicely for the scalar examples we will look at later, as we have the same motion in the picking hand here as we have in a three notes per string scalar movement. This exercise is made slightly easier by the fact that we are using less movement in the fretting hand.

Essentially for each arpeggio you will start on the root note, playing down up down, then go to the major third on the next string, playing up down up. This is exactly the sort of problem we will encounter when using scalar shapes, so it's really good that you are getting exposed to it in this sort of way now. Of the exercises covered so far, this is by far and away the most demanding, as always, take your time with it and don't move on until you've got it sorted.

Example 25

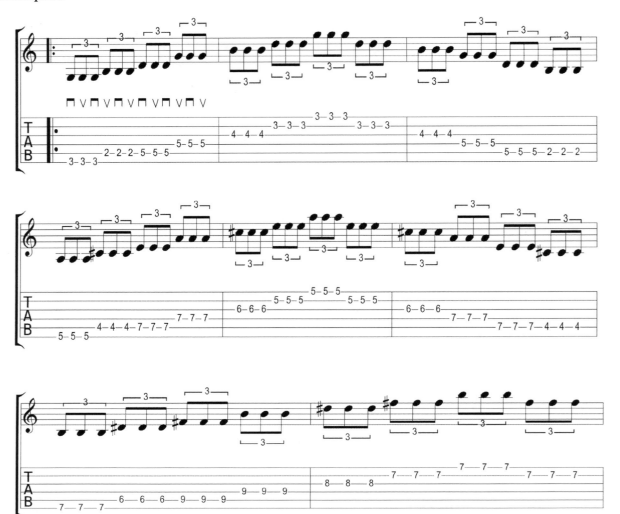

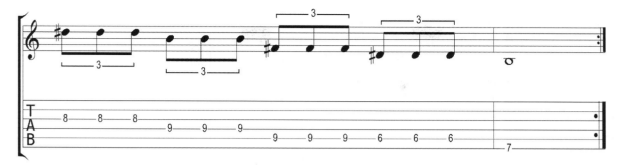

There is one last arpeggio style example I would like to share with you before we move on to some scalar examples. Example 26 shows how you can use arpeggios to create a rhythm guitar part, a bit like Jason Becker used to do. Where Jason would opt for a sweep picking approach, which is more common for arpeggios, we are actually going to use this idea for our alternate picking.

Once again it is because it gives you lots of mileage for string crossing, but also it's showing you a way that you can musically employ this sort of thing. All of the arpeggios in the example are from the key of C major, and are outlining a chord progression. The progression we are outlining is C, G, Am, Em, F, G, C. Essentially, instead of playing straight chords, we are playing the arpeggio (as an arpeggio is the notes of a chord, broken up) to give us a different texture.

Try working this idea into your own music, you may like the results. Of course, you may wish to compose your own etudes based on this idea for your own practice, or even better, parts for your own songs.

Example 26

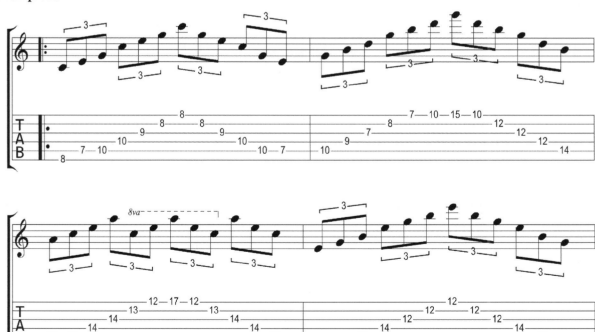

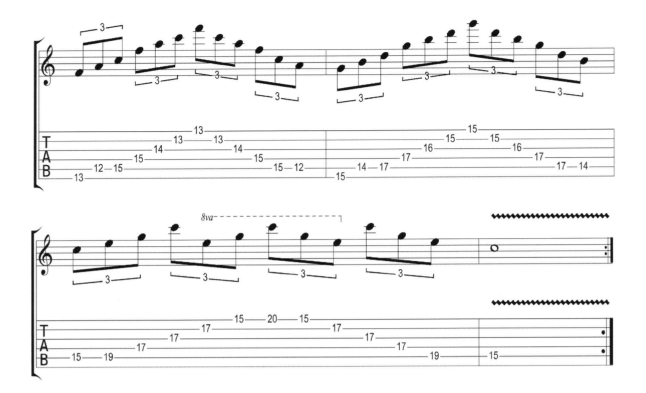

I think that should be enough arpeggio based ideas to keep you busy for a while. Don't forget that you should be practising these ideas in different keys and with different positions if possible. Use ideas like the last example to create your own licks, sequences and etudes for practice and, of course, parts for songs.

What we are going to take a look at next is some examples based on scalar ideas rather than arpeggio based examples. In Book One, we looked at the five CAGED positions of the major/natural minor scale, but for our purposes now we will be using the three notes per string variations from our legato chapter.

The three notes per string variations of the scale are the most common approach for technical work by modern rock and fusion guitarists. Whether you favour the legato or the picking approach, three notes per string is the way to go when looking to play longer flowing lines. Now that your fretting hand is proficient at playing three notes per string legato ideas, it should now be easier to bed in a good facility for alternate picking concepts.

The following examples are all written in position five of the C major scale. This is because it is in a nice area of the neck to begin playing through all seven positions. For example, if you practise the sequences where they are written, in position five, and then continue through all seven positions until you reach the octave of position five, you will have spanned a nice portion of the neck which is friendly to your fingers. I would urge you to play these exercises in position four in its lowest position also, but perhaps not to start with, as it is a tricky area in terms of fingering.

Essentially though the idea I am pointing to is that it doesn't really matter where I have written the example, once you have learned it, you will need to practise it in all seven shapes, and then practise it in all twelve keys for you to have the optimum knowledge of the fretboard. Not just from a technical perspective, but also a theoretical perspective. This all relates back to my point in Book One about how you need to be able to see where the notes are on the neck, and also have the technical facility to be able to play them. Being able to play in all twelve keys is vital, so don't skim over certain keys.

The first scalar example we will look at is a common sequencing idea. We are playing the C major scale position five in groups of four. So you will play up four notes from the first note of the shape (in this case a G), then you will come back to the second note of the shape (A) and ascend another four notes. You do this until you have reached the last note for that shape.

Remember to use some sort of timekeeping device, such as a metronome, a drum machine or a backing track which you have slowed to a sufficient enough pace for you to be able to keep a strict sixteenth note rhythmic pulse. When you can play the exercise fully with no mistakes you can then start pushing the speed limit up, but don't try to go too fast too quickly.

If you can play this sort of thing to around 160 bpm you have reached what is known as a standard top speed for this kind of idea. I would recommend getting the exercise under your fingers really slowly, away from a metronome at first, to bed in the exercise. Then once it's under your fingers, begin playing it with a metronome at a comfortable tempo. Around 60 bpm would be a good starting point. Example 27 shows the ascending version of this exercise in position five and Example 28 shows the descending version. Remember that you should always be strictly alternate picking, otherwise it will defeat the object of the exercise.

Example 27

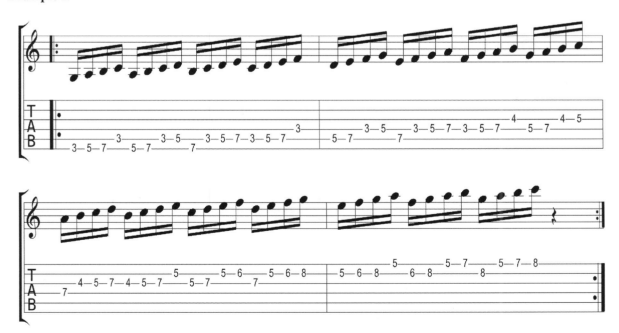

Example 28

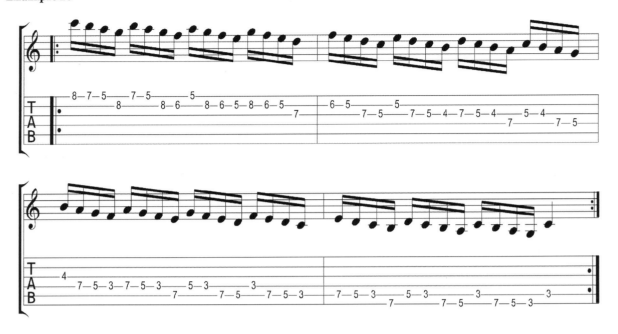

Example 29 shows a different pattern for the principal group of four sequences. What you will do now is play up three notes of the scale shape, then back to your first note, and carry on in such a way. You're still ascending in rhythmic groupings of four but you are placing different notes on the beat, which gives you a completely different sounding exercise to the previous ones.

Example 29

Example 30 meanwhile shows the first bar of the descending form for this pattern. I'm sure you can work out how the rest goes by now.

Example 30
Continue through shape

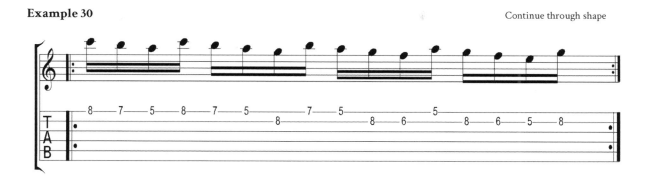

Example 31 shows another pattern for ascending the scales in groups of four. This time we start by playing an interval of a third, which means from the first note you play you will go up three notes on the scale to play the next note, then you will descend the scale back to the first note you played. From there the pattern will continue from the second note of the scale and so on until you have completed the shape you are playing.

Example 31
Continue through shape

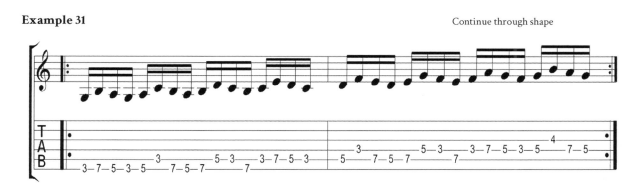

Example 32 shows the first two bars of the descending version of Example 31. Make sure you play through the whole shape though; the two bars written are just to give you an example of the sequence. Once you have two bars the rest should be self-explanatory. As always make sure you're practising these ideas in all seven positions and in all twelve keys. That way there is enough to keep you busy for a very long time.

Example 32
Continue through shape

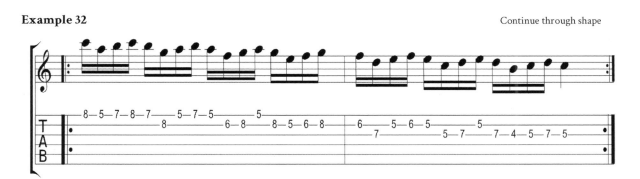

We are now going to look at playing scales in intervallic leaps rather than patterns. Playing in intervallic leaps is very good for us for several reasons. It helps our ears to be able to hear different intervals, for transcribing and improvisation purposes. It also helps with our fretboard knowledge, as you will become much more familiar with where the intervals are on the neck, and finally, some of the interval leaps provide us with some very difficult picking indeed, so they are brilliant for our technique.

The first interval we are looking at is thirds. What this means is we are going to play through a scale shape in diatonic (which means only notes belonging to the scale) interval leaps of a third. So for example if you start on a G, your next note from the C major scale will be a B, three notes higher. You will play this throughout a whole scale shape as in Example 33. Don't forget that although I have written this only in ascending form, there is a descending version too, so make sure you play it both ways, and as always in all shapes and keys.

Example 33

Example 34 shows the ascending scale in interval leaps of fourths. This is particularly tricky as in the fretting hand you have to do lots of rolling. You can't just barre the notes as you will get lots of note bleed, which sounds extremely annoying, especially on heavily distorted tones. Also, the outside the string alternate picking is pretty intense here, it's very difficult to pick all the way through the whole shape without making a single mistake, but that's what you're aiming to do.

Example 34

OK, now let's take a look at fifths. These once again are particularly difficult and present all the same problems as fourths. There is lots of outside the string picking and there is also lots of fretting hand rolling. Your two hands will need to be perfectly synced in order to play the notes cleanly. It's a very demanding interval so take your time, not just from a technique perspective but also from a fretboard knowledge perspective. It's quite hard to 'see' where you need to be playing, the bigger the interval leaps are getting.

Example 35

Now we are going to look at leaps of sixths, which are now getting really tricky. There isn't any barring to worry about this time but there is lots of string skipping, which makes it quite difficult to maintain strict alternate picking. Your picking hand will most likely want to pick in the direction of the string it is making a big jump to. You will need to be disciplined and keep the pick moving in an alternate fashion. If you can alternate pick big interval leaps, then standard scalar stuff will become easy! Be careful in your fretting hand too as this is quite hard to fret.

Example 36

Our final interval and also our last alternate picking example for Book Two is the interval of a seventh. These are the biggest leaps we can make before going into the next octave. As you can imagine they are extremely difficult for both hands, and also as they are so big it's very hard to see them on the neck. Take your time with these. Remember it's not about speed, but accuracy.

Example 37

In this chapter, we have greatly expanded our ability to alternate pick, and have learned how to incorporate lots of ideas for arpeggio and scalar playing into our music. As always it is now your job to really hone these new skills to a highly polished and sharpened level, so that you may begin creating music with these ideas.

Try coming up with some cool rhythm guitar parts that utilize the arpeggio style ideas we have looked at. To do this, either write a chord progression, or use a progression from a song you really like, and try arpeggiating it using the alternate picking technique. You may love the results, you may not. You will not know until you try it out.

Also, from a lead guitar perspective, try adding in some of the new intervallic style playing we looked at into your runs and solos. This new way of playing will change your sound quite drastically. Add a few string bending exits to these too and you may come up with some pretty cool licks!

In the next chapter, we will look at taking picking hand technique further with the advanced sweep picking technique.

CHAPTER 3

Sweep Picking

In this chapter we will be looking at three string sweeping. In Book One we have looked at using the sweeping motion over more strings, however, the examples in this chapter are far more musical, and are using triad shapes that actually fit together to form the basis of proper licks. Sweep picking lends itself very well to playing licks based on major or minor triads, and can be found all over the playing of most modern rock, fusion and jazz guitarists.

The particular style of sweeping we will be looking at in this chapter is most commonly associated with Swedish neoclassical rock player Yngwie Malmsteen, but don't be put off by this technique if you don't favour Yngwie's playing. The ideas presented here can be used in many different genres, for example, lots of fusion guitarists use sweep picking when they are superimposing arpeggios to get real nice jazzy licks.

I would recommend taking a listen to fusion players such as Frank Gambale and also YouTube phenomenon, Alex Hutchings. Both have a wonderful facility for sweep picking. Frank Gambale is also the godfather of the economy picking technique, which is essentially scalar sweeping, so he is a must-hear guitar player.

Mastering three string sweeps and seeing how you can make the licks fit together is an essential building block to being able to create bigger licks over more strings, so we need to make sure we are very comfortable with three strings before moving on to more strings. Sweeping over more strings and larger arpeggio shapes is covered in the third book of this series, as sweeping full arpeggios is a virtuosic technique. The art of sweeping is very difficult to master and may not feel natural for you to play in this way, but you must persevere in order to open up lots of musical possibilities.

If you can do it and then decide that it's not for you, that's fine. I always maintain though that you should master a technique first before deciding that it's not right for you. You wouldn't want to miss out on playing some really cool licks, or have an incredible sound in your head that you just can't get onto the guitar, purely because you haven't put in the required time to have the technique.

When you sweep arpeggios in an ascending manner, you must make sure that you push through the string you're playing, so that the pick lands on the next string. In Book One, I used the analogy of park railings and a stick. If you drag a stick through park railings it pings onto and lands on the next rail, before bending backwards and then pings onto the next again. Your pick should have the same movement on the strings, and try to make it do so when performing these licks.

On your descending licks the pick needs to be dragged through the strings, once again so it lands on the next string to be played. When sweeping through any arpeggio the motion should be nice and fluid, so make sure there are no jerky movements of the wrist. One thing that will help is if you angle your wrist in the direction that you are moving. For example, when sweeping an ascending arpeggio, your wrist should be angled down, which will mean the pick is angled away from the strings, therefore creating less resistance. When playing descending, your wrist should be angled upwards for the same reasons. This kind of creates an imaginary figure of eight with the pick.

Bear in mind that the fretting hand has a lot of work to do with sweeping, although it's predominantly a picking hand technique. Sometimes with sweeping you have lots of rolling to do as one finger may need to fret several strings. This is hard to master and hard to sync up both hands correctly, so make sure you aren't getting lots of horrible note bleed from improper fretting hand technique.

On any arpeggio types that don't require you to use rolling, make sure you only have one finger on the fretboard at any one time. Otherwise you will hear a chord sound rather than a single note arpeggio. If you have more than one finger on the fretboard at any one time with this technique, it sounds awful when there is a lot of distortion coming from the amp, so be very aware that all of your muting and fretting hand accuracy is just as good as your picking hand technique.

The last point I would like to make before we take a look at any musical examples is that you should really have the triad arpeggios well drilled before you start trying to play these examples. Going back to my point in Book One about seeing where to go on the neck and also technically being able to play the ideas, you will certainly find it a lot easier to play ideas that link the arpeggios together if you already know their position on the fretboard, so if you're not quite comfortable with that yet, go back to Book One and study the shapes, then begin looking at the examples.

Example 38 is a position one A minor triad sweeping lick across three strings. This is what we call a static lick, as you are just playing up and down the one inversion of the arpeggio. Follow the pick directions written in the example and you will see there is an alternate picking motion on the top string, and then you sweep through the shape back to the top string where you alternate pick again. Later we will look at using a pull-off with this kind of idea.

Example 38

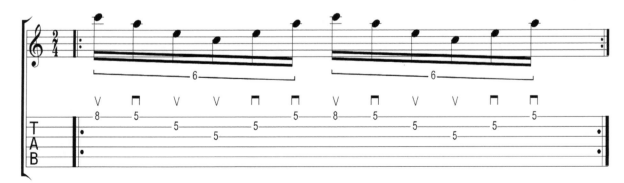

Example 39 shows the fingering for a position three A minor triad, another common place on the neck for this type of idea to be found. The fingering for this shape would be to start with your fourth finger, then first finger, second finger, first finger again and then reverse back to the top. It's interesting that the chord shape from the CAGED system that this arpeggio is from is rarely used because of the difficult fingering, but the arpeggio is very commonly used.

Example 39

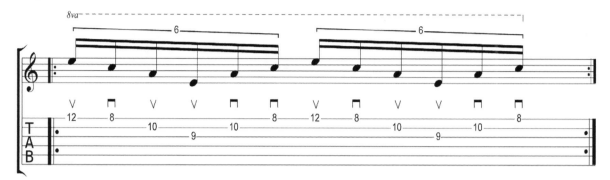

Example 40 shows the position four A minor triad shape from the CAGED system. Once again this is another very common sweep shape but has the added difficulty of being quite stretchy in the fretting hand. Use fingers 4, 1, 2 then 3 for this lick.

Example 40

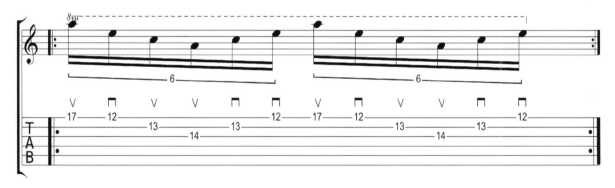

Examples 41, 42 and 43 all show fingerings for G major arpeggios. So not only now will we have different shapes, as the major arpeggios have a major third as opposed to the minor triad's minor third, but I've also written the major arpeggios with a pull-off on the top string. So far we have looked at using a bit of alternate picking combined with the sweep. This time you will pick the top string with an upstroke, pull-off to your next note of the arpeggio and then continue sweeping through.

On the ascending version you will find that you sweep down, then reverse to an upstroke, pull-off then keep going. Both ways to play the arpeggios are valid, but I think once you have tried both you should find whichever way suits you best and then stick with that. Example 41 shows position one G major.

Example 41

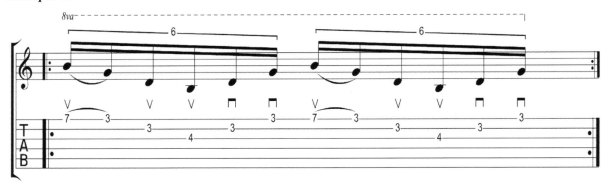

Example 42 shows the position three G major arpeggio. Use the same technique as Example 41.

Example 42

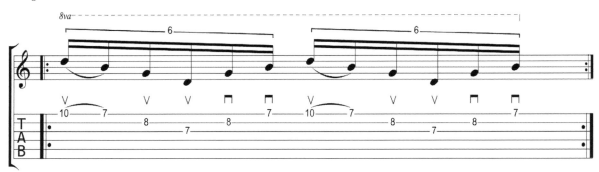

Example 43 shows the position four fingering for G major. Use your second finger for the twelfth fret notes, which means you need to employ the rolling technique.

Example 43

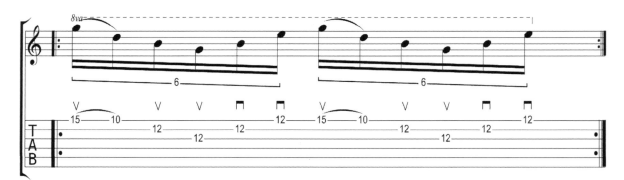

Now that we have looked at all the common individual shapes for major and minor arpeggios in their three string guise, I would suggest that you need to spend a fair amount of time just playing up and down each one, gradually building your speed to higher tempos and making sure you have totally grasped where they all live on the neck. Once you are comfortable playing each shape technically, and know where it is on the neck relative to the other shapes, you can begin looking at the next group of examples which link them together.

Example 44 then is an extended A minor arpeggio lick that combines shapes one, two and three. Linking the shapes in this way gives you much longer arpeggio phrases and is very reminiscent of the playing of neoclassical rockers such as Yngwie Malmsteen and Jason Becker. For this example, I have added an exit idea. I've used a bend with tone wide rock vibrato to sound stylistically accurate. An exit such as this makes this example go from being an exercise to an exciting neoclassical lick.

Example 44

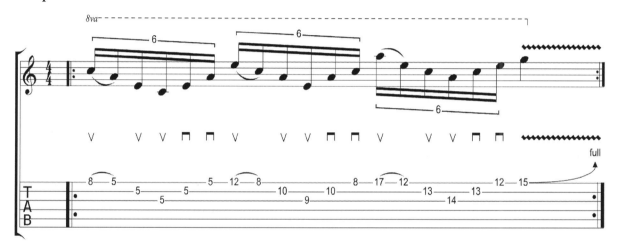

Example 45 shows how you would connect the G major shapes in a similar fashion.

Example 45

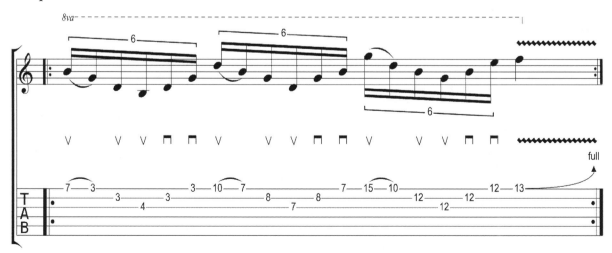

Example 46 shows the fingering for diminished arpeggios used by Yngwie Malmsteen. These arpeggios form a big part of Yngwie's style, but can also be used in any other genre that uses diminished arpeggios. For example, Guthrie Govan has used licks such as this in his jazz band The Fellowship. When players are fans of all types of music, the licks they glean from one style can very often cross over into others, which is how we create fusion music. Even if you don't like rock and metal, there will be places for licks such as this in your music, try and work it in and see what results you get. Use a fingering of 4-1-2-3 for these arpeggios to play them in the same way that Yngwie does.

Example 46

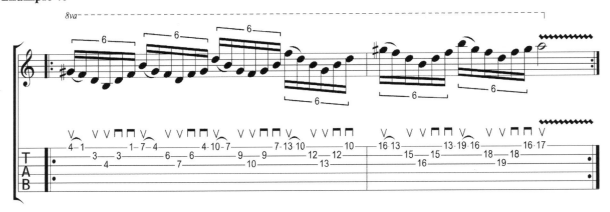

Example 47 is based on the song 'Demon Driver' by Yngwie Malmsteen. Essentially what this example is showing you is how you can follow chord progressions when playing arpeggio sequences. It's a very demanding exercise that covers a lot of ground on the neck, and also the fact that Yngwie usually plays this kind of thing at the speed of light causes difficulties for the rest of us. Take your time with this one as it is so demanding in both the picking hand and the fretting hand. Play the lick very slowly for a continuous amount of time before applying any speed. Only when the notes of the example have become familiar is any speed recommended.

Example 47

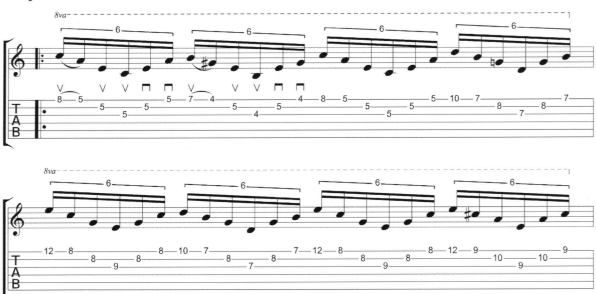

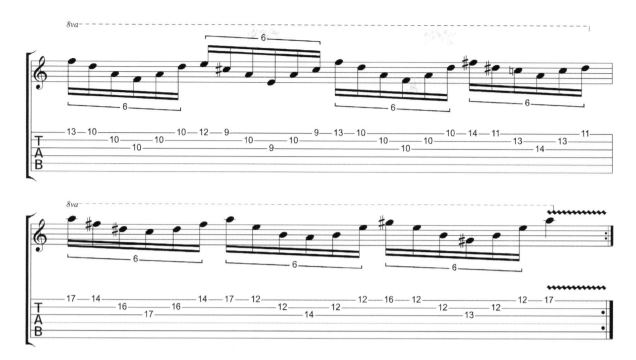

Example 48 is an extended major arpeggio run that is very reminiscent of the sort of thing Jason Becker may have done. Jason was an absolutely amazing guitarist accomplished in all techniques, but his command of arpeggios and the sweeping technique was truly second to none. If you haven't heard his album *Perpetual Burn* it is a must for any guitarist that wants to know about blistering technique.

Example 48

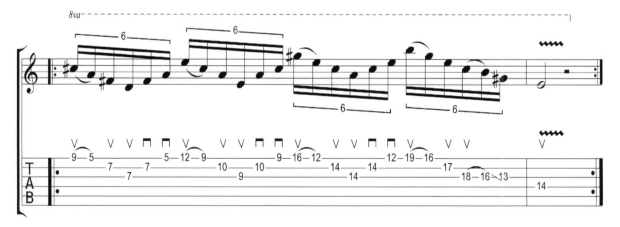

Example 49 is a very challenging lick that I accidentally came across when looking at Irish folk music. A few years ago a great guitarist friend of mine went to see the Riverdance show, and became hooked on Irish music. He began transcribing the parts for the guitar, and shared his transcriptions with me. We both became very impressed with the level of virtuosity there was in this style of music, and also just how tough it was to play on the guitar.

The example I've written is a lick that is commonly used in this style of music. It's based on a D shaped chord for A major, which I would finger with the second, third and first fingers from the first to the third string. Then what you do is move the root note on the second string up to the twelfth fret and the major third on the first string up to the tenth fret. This now means the intervals you have are the fifth, second and fourth (suspended arpeggio) rather than the original fifth, root and third (major arpeggio). As far as the pick directions are concerned it will be down, up, up throughout. This kind of idea is very uncommon for guitarists and is really tricky to get down so you will need to take your time with it. You will have to admit there is something cool about its unusual sound. If you like ideas like this try transcribing music not commonly associated with the guitar, it can give you some awesome ideas.

Example 49

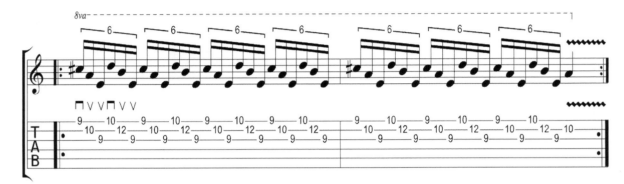

Getting back to a more rock friendly approach, Example 50 is more the sort of thing you would find in the band Cacophony's repertoire. So far we have looked a lot at Yngwie Malmsteen's approach to sweeping, but Cacophony, who were comprised of guitar duo Jason Becker and Megadeth legend Marty Friedman, are also a very special act when it comes to this technique. Cacophony came from the same Shrapnel Records era as Yngwie in the 1980s. This was the golden age of virtuoso guitar playing.

The astonishing thing with Cacophony is that they were a duo, able to play everything in sync, and play harmonies with this crazy level of ability. The exercise follows a chord progression; Dm, G, Am, F, G, Am. Over a progression like this the band would use arpeggios very much like a rhythm guitar part. Check out their albums *Speed Metal Symphony* or *Go Off!* for lots of this kind of playing.

Example 50

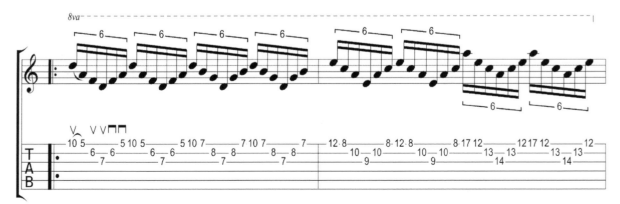

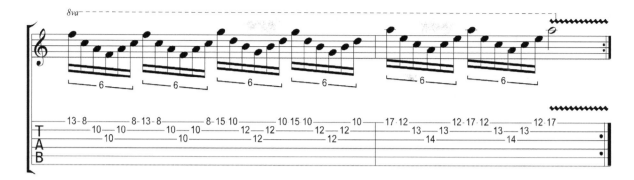

For our last sweeping example, I want to move slightly away from the rock side of things and look at how jazz and fusion guitarists can use arpeggios to get their sound. Technically how you play the arpeggios is fundamentally the same, it's just the way that they are used that gives us different genre specifics. In our rock examples we have been either playing one arpeggio in different inversions, or we have basically played the correct arpeggio that fits the underlying chord progression. Jazzers like to superimpose different or 'wrong' arpeggios over certain chords in order to get extended sounds and outline different modes or scales.

In Example 51 we are looking at using G and F major triads over a G7 chord in order to get a nice G Mixolydian modal sound. If you are unaware of modes check out some music theory to understand what they are, but essentially the best way to describe them is that modes are different sounds, or different flavours that can be created when we play a straight major scale from different points. Normally you play C major from C to C. If however you play it from G to G you get the sound of G Mixolydian. Mixolydian is a favourite among jazz, rock and blues guitarists as it has a really cool major and minor ambiguity about it.

Our example is based on the player Frank Gambale. We will be looking at how he would superimpose the two different triads over the G7 to get this modal sound. He is of course the obvious choice for this technique as he invented economy picking (or as he calls it, 'speed picking'), which is the scalar version of sweeping, and he is a terrifyingly good sweep picker. Check out Frank's tunes '6.8 Shaker' from the album *Passages*, and 'Naughty Business' from the album *The Great Explorers* for lots of scary technique and Mixolydian soloing.

Example 51

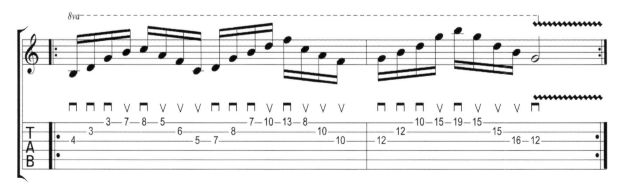

In this chapter we really have taken this technique to the next level. The examples we have looked at are in the style of some of the most accomplished professional guitar players on the planet, and making these licks work for you will be no easy task. Spend plenty of time playing through the licks slowly, getting a good feel for them and also making the sound of these arpeggio based phrases familiar in your inner ear. Once you have these concepts down, try and incorporate these examples into your own music and also try and come up with lots of your own sweeping licks.

Take a good listen to the players mentioned in this chapter to hear how they use sweep picking in their own unique style, but also listen to lots of other famous guitarists from rock, jazz and fusion genres. You will be surprised at how much this technique plays a part in their soloing ideas. Once you're comfortable with sweeping, head on to the next chapter where we will take a look at the tapping technique.

CHAPTER 4

Tapping

Tapping has certainly become synonymous with shred guitar, since Eddie Van Halen burst on to the scene back in the late '70s. Due to its association with hair metal and a showing off approach to guitar playing, this technique has managed to get itself a very bad rep. It is, however, a very important technique in the modern guitar style, and when used musically is capable of giving us some truly beautiful sounding results.

In Book One of this series, we looked at getting started with this technique. We also looked at using tapping as an extension of our legato examples rather than an entirely new technique. Legato is the use of hammer-ons and pull-offs, and tapping is essentially hammering and pulling off with extra fingers from the picking hand.

The technique is nothing more than a means to an end. It allows us to play much wider intervals than you can reach with the humble stretch of your fretting hand. It also allows us to play certain passages much faster than any other technique. The thing with tapping is it doesn't have to just be about speed and blowing audiences away with visually impressive licks, we can get some wonderful and creative sounds from tapping.

In our first stage of tapping from Book One, we looked at lots of static licks, and incorporating more notes in the fretting hand from our major scale rather than just straight pentatonic licks. In this book, we are going to be looking at licks that cover more strings, and also moving licks around the neck a lot more so we can start creating runs and lengthier tapped passages.

This selection of tapping examples have been designed to show you how to break out of playing straight arpeggios on one string, as this is the sort of thing that tapping gets its bad rep from. It can sound very linear and quite boring just to hear someone playing an arpeggio over and over again at high speed, so what we are looking at here is how to get that nice bubbly and smooth legato effect with our tapping licks, so that this technique can start bringing a distinctive new flavour to your solos.

Before we get started we should just have a recap of how best to perform the technique, as some of the principles we looked at with the static ideas in Book One won't hold up the same when we are moving around the neck. The biggest problem we face when tapping is how to keep the idle strings muted, as once we remove the picking hand from its position near the bridge, we lose the ability to palm mute idle bass strings.

When tapping, have your hand set up so that the palm of your picking hand still comes across the strings at whatever point on the guitar you are currently playing. It will help to keep you locked in to this position by hooking your fourth and third finger of your picking hand around the bottom of the guitar's neck. You can only really keep both of these fingers hooked around the neck when you're playing on the first, second and third strings, when you move to lower strings you will need to release the third finger and use your fourth finger to keep you in position.

As far as moving around the neck is concerned you just slide the picking hand around as you would the fretting hand. Keeping the karate chop part of your palm muting the idle bass strings is essential, especially when playing with high gain, as this needs to be controlled in order to get rid of nasty and unwanted feedback. You will be able to keep hold of your pick in its standard grip if you use the second finger for doing all of the tapping. It makes sense to keep hold of the pick as you would normally, so that you can more easily make the transition between tapped runs, alternate and sweep picking to allow you to be as versatile as possible.

Like anything with the guitar it is a case of practising the ideas and playing around with them until you find exactly what fits for you and your own unique style. If you use the ideas I have stated here as a guide you will find that you can mute, manoeuvre around the neck and get the best tone. Our first example for the tapping technique is a position one minor pentatonic lick, but is going to be a really fluid hyper speed fusion lick in the style of players like Greg Howe.

You are tapping all of your notes at the twelfth fret, as these are all notes that belong to the key of A minor, and then playing a straight minor pentatonic scale in the fretting hand. However, the lick is being played in septuplets (seven notes per beat) which are very demanding. You may wish to practise each string individually, and then build up to playing string pairs before trying to do the whole lick in one go. The transitions between strings are particularly difficult so make sure you are getting this right.

Example 52

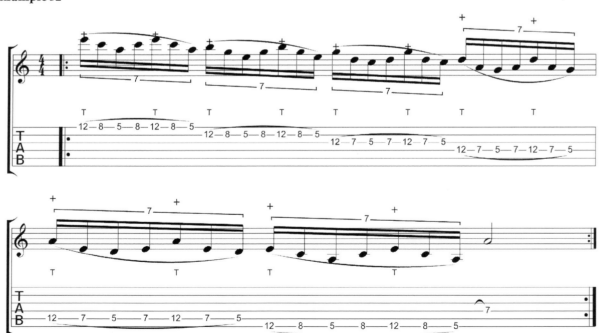

Example 53 is another pentatonic lick but this time what we are doing is combining notes from two positions. The lick is played in the key of D minor and is using positions one and two of the D minor pentatonic scale. In your fretting hand you will be playing the standard position one shape, but your picking hand will be alternating between playing position two and position one notes. This example makes use of fretting hand tapping, which is executed by hammering a note on a string with your fretting hand where no previous note has been played. Fretting hand tapping is denoted by a slur marking between two different strings.

Example 53

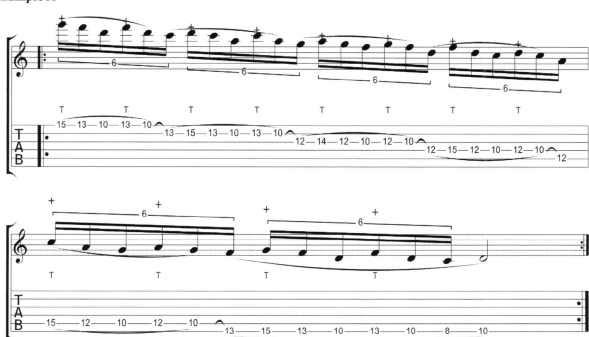

Example 54 is another pentatonic example but this time we are looking at taking a lick along the neck, through all the CAGED positions. In Book One, we looked at a super fast trill idea that players like Billy Sheehan and Paul Gilbert use to get an outrageous hammer-on and pull-off speed lick. It's a lick where you are trilling with your fretting hand but you're also doubling up the trill with a tap from the picking hand too, so the notes are flying out all over the place.

With this example you perform the same super trill idea but you do it for one beat in all five positions of A minor pentatonic on the first string. It's a very nice bubbly sounding lick that is also very impressive visually and will turn a lot of heads. The fortunate thing is that for all the advanced sound you get, it falls under the fingers nicely as the pentatonic is so familiar.

Example 54

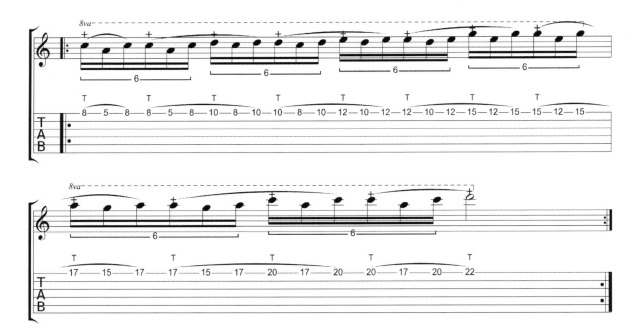

Example 55 is a wide interval lick that would be impossible to play at this speed and fluidity without tapping. Essentially you are playing a standard string crossing lick, once again with all notes from A minor pentatonic in your fretting hand, and you are tapping notes from the A natural minor scale. You could make this a complete pentatonic idea, but I've kept the tapping hand playing the same frets on each string so that it's an easier lick to familiarize yourself with. By all means experiment with different approaches that sound cool to you though.

Example 55

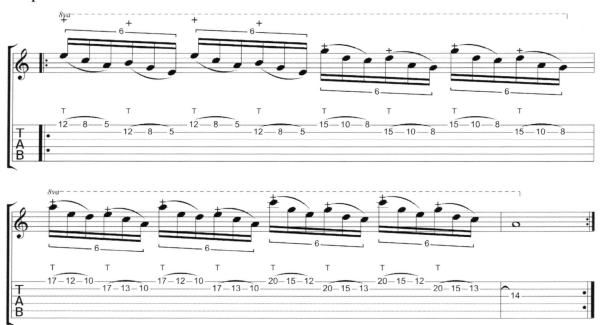

Example 56 is based on the introduction to Eddie Van Halen's famous track 'Hot For Teacher'. It's an arpeggio based lick that is using not only taps but pull-offs to open strings, which is a really musical way to use this feature of the guitar. This approach also demonstrates a new way for you to incorporate the fast arpeggio ideas we saw in the sweep picking section if you're not a fan of the sweep technique.

You may indeed prefer the smooth tone of these arpeggios. As long as you have tried both ways I think it's valid for you to lean to a preferred way to play, as long as you're not shunning a style because you can't do it. The arpeggios being played here are; Am, Dm and G, so try sweeping the same thing and see which way you prefer.

Example 56

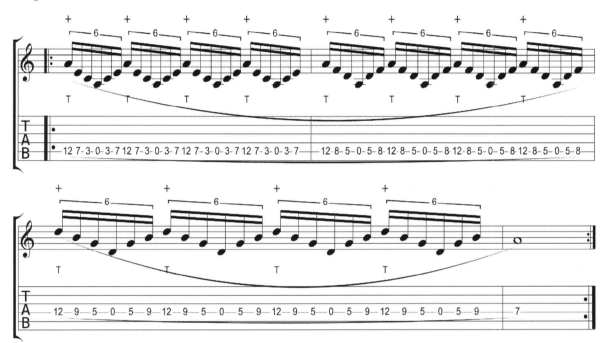

Example 57 is a similar idea to that found in Joe Satriani's tune 'Always With Me, Always With You'. Essentially what we are doing here is tapping a G at the twelfth fret on the G string, and then moving throughout the G Mixolydian mode that we talked about in the sweep picking examples. This means we are using the C major scale that we are familiar with but looking at it from G as the root note.

With this sort of idea, you can keep your picking hand in the locked position but be careful that you are not muting the open string that we want to hear. Just use one finger on the fretting hand and let it move around the neck to fret the notes. I'm sure you will agree this gives us a really interesting texture.

Example 57

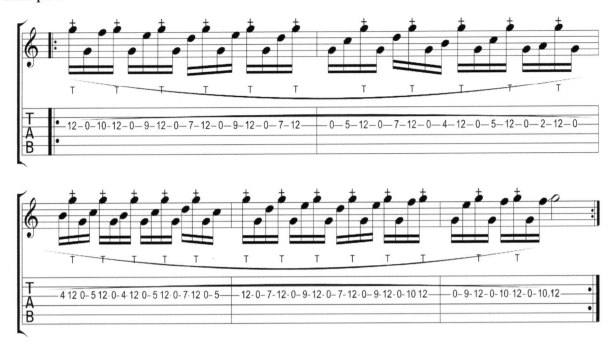

Example 58 is our last of the open string tapping examples, and is a lick that is inspired by a lick in the Andy Timmons' track 'Ghost of You'. Once again you are tapping statically at the twelfth fret on the G string, and moving a couple of shapes around the neck to get different sounds from the Mixolydian mode. The exit of the lick has a really nice country vibe to it, try the idea with your own music though and see how you can make it fit for you. Hint, can you make this work with other interesting sounding scales?

Example 58

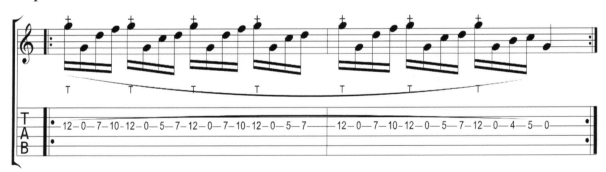

Going back to Example 56's idea of moving from sweeping to tapping, I'd like to show you some tapping ideas that give you similar sounds to the sweeping ideas we have looked at. Tapping can give us an excellent facility to play arpeggio based phrases, so if you're not keen on sweeping then tapping could be your answer to getting fast arpeggios into your music.

Nuno Bettencourt from the band Extreme likes to use this idea a lot, so you're in good company if you favour this way of playing. In the example, we have a neoclassical style chord progression, which is outlining an Am-E-Am movement. This chord progression is what we call a V-I (five one) perfect cadence, and comes from the harmonic minor scale which has a very distinctive neoclassical tonality. As far as the technique is concerned, these are standard tapped arpeggios with the same sort of technique we looked at in Book One. Your picking hand will remain rooted at the twelfth fret whilst the fretting hand is doing all the position shifting.

Example 59

Keeping with our neoclassical theme, Example 60 is very much inspired by Yngwie Malmsteen in terms of the arpeggios we are using. However, where of course Yngwie would be sweeping this idea, we are going to be tapping it. I've reverted back to a sixteenth note feel for this one, so each arpeggio will be played in ascending and descending form. When you get to the upper reaches of tempo for this idea, it really can be played at super high speeds. I'd like to think that the classical masters themselves would be impressed hearing these ideas played on a distorted electric guitar. The chord progression we are following once again is in the key of A minor and follows; Am, B diminished, G# diminished, Am, F, Dm, Em, C.

Example 60

For our final tapping example, I want to take a look at something that's not arpeggio based, and also doesn't sound particularly scalar either. This is an idea that phenomenal tapper Greg Howe has used to get really interesting intervallic sounds. Essentially we are using our A minor pentatonic scale as a scaffold, but this lick doesn't really sound pentatonic at all due to the nature of the interval leaps of fifths.

This kind of idea sounds really bubbly at high speed and has a wonderful fusion quality about it, this is due to the angular nature of the intervals. Technically this one is pretty difficult due to the fact a lot of the time you are 'hammering on from nowhere', which is how Greg describes his take on the tapping technique. Essentially fretting hand tapping is what Greg describes here, so for example, the third note of the lick will be produced by you hammering on to the seventh fret of the fifth string when no previous note has been played on that string.

The term 'hammering from nowhere' comes from the fact that usually you have played a note, or a note is ringing on a string before you perform a hammer-on. Fretting hand taps require lots of accuracy and they also require quite a decent amount of force to be able to work. It takes a fair bit of time to master but now you have worked your way through all these other tapping and legato examples, your fretting hand should be more than capable.

Example 61

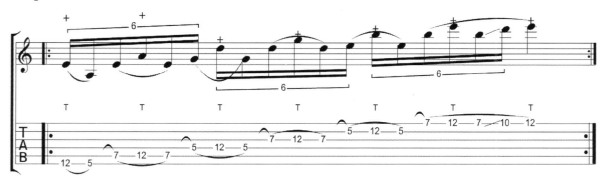

In the previous chapter, we have expanded the tapping technique by looking at more complex ideas for pentatonic and arpeggio based ideas. These concepts make up the bulk of lead guitar style tapping in the professional world, and you will be able to play quite a serious amount of modern rock and fusion style licks once you have these examples mastered.

Make sure to get each example fully under the fingers before applying any speed, and as always try to find places in your music where you can see these ideas fitting. If your music taste doesn't require the blistering lead approach that is normally associated with tapping, you may certainly be able to find some really melodic, wide stretch licks that you couldn't possibly play without your new tapping skill. Experiment a lot and I'm sure you will find plenty of musical ways to use this technique. If you find yourself stuck for inspiration, take a listen to anything by Eddie Van Halen, Greg Howe and Guthrie Govan to see how this technique can be used to amazing effect in all genres of music.

In the next chapter we will be looking at how we can develop our speed to play at pro level tempos.

CHAPTER 5

Developing Speed

One question that every student has asked me at some point is: 'How does that guitarist play so fast?'

At this stage you should have quite a good technical grasp of the guitar. You also probably feel quite comfortable on the instrument, tackling more difficult solos and not being afraid of learning harder passages. You may feel though that in spite of the fact that you can play some cool tapping or sweep picked licks, there is still a gap between your own level and pro level in terms of speed. You may find it really difficult to learn certain passages and when you're improvising, you may be hearing fast fluid runs in your head that you wish to play, but your fingers just won't keep up.

In this chapter, we will look to address this problem of speed, and look at some ways in which you can work on all of the exercises in this book that will yield good results for you. Firstly, make sure you have your metronome handy, as you will certainly need this for the following ideas. The best kind of exercises for working purely on speed development, are cycled licks. Taking a single cell idea and drilling it out, in order to force your fingers to move faster, is a great way to build speed. Let's take Example 12 from our Legato chapter as an excellent foundation for building speed.

When I first started using this exercise, I found I was extremely poor at it. Using my first, third and fourth fingers were a particular combination I wasn't fond of, and I found this lick extremely challenging. At first I was only capable of playing this lick at around 60 bpm in sixteenth note triplets. After hours of work I was able to build this lick up to around 140 bpm. Here's how I did it.

Firstly, you need to have the notes very much embedded in your fingers and the mind. If your mind is too occupied with which notes to play next, this slows you down immensely. What you need, is for the notes to be second nature, so you have them so ingrained that you don't even need to think about them. To get to this point, I played the lick continuously at 60 bpm for around 30 minutes a day for a whole week.

At the same time, I was of course practising lots of other exercises, for similar durations. After that week's solid practice, the notes were in my mind and under my fingers, and I was ready to begin building speed. I figured that the next logical step would be to put the metronome up to 70 bpm. I tried playing the lick and pretty much instantly failed. I couldn't believe how difficult the 10 bpm jump was.

I stuck at this for a few minutes before deciding it was too hard. So I thought I'd try 66 bpm. Magically, this felt really easy. All of a sudden I was playing 6 bpm faster than my original tempo and finding it OK. I had discovered that if you push yourself way beyond your limit and struggle for long enough, that when you bring the tempo down to just above where you were, you would find it easy.

This idea is extremely similar to a 'shocking principle' used in the gym for building muscles. Essentially the idea is to try to lift a weight that is far too big for you, and then when you lower the weight down to just above your maximum lift, you should find it easier. Therefore, that new weight now becomes your new maximum lift.

In my quest to further build my tempo with this same lick, I would use the metronome in different ways and go up in different increments depending on what felt comfortable. Increments of 6 and 4 bpm I have found to be very useful. The interesting thing is that if you go up 6 bpm on one round of the lick, and then 4 bpm on another, this means that in two rounds you have gone up 10 bpm.

Every now and then it is a good idea to try a significant jump, such as 10 bpm, when you are rising through the metronome, just to see how you get on. You may find that at certain points that 10 bpm jump isn't too difficult and you can make it. You need to give yourself time to bed in a new tempo if it's much higher than your previous one. Usually I would say to my students that you need to practise an exercise for around five minutes before trying to bump up your speed again. The duration you need to play an exercise for is dependent on the increment in which you advance on the metronome.

If you're making big jumps of 10 bpm each time you perform an exercise, then you will need to give yourself more time at each tempo to allow it to settle in to your fingers. If, however, you are going up in increments of 3 to 4 bpm, you will need to spend less time playing each exercise before going up again. In the most extreme cases of difficulty I use a method that I call the 'one minute method'. I used this to great effect on my sweep picking licks when studying for my grade eight exam. As a part of that exam, I had to play a sweep picking study and also there was quite a long arpeggio section in one of my pieces, which I wasn't particularly good at.

To improve this section, I employed the one minute method for the first time, and it worked wonders. What you first need to do is find a tempo that you can play a given exercise at comfortably. Once you have found that tempo, time yourself playing it for one minute to your metronome or drum machine. You will find that certain metronome apps have practice timers on them, which help you a bit more in this quest. I used a stopwatch, as these apps didn't exist then, but on certain apps they will count down the minute for you and stop ticking when your time is done.

Once your minute is up, you need to rest for one minute. Whilst resting, put your metronome up one beat per minute. At the end of the one minute rest, play the lick again solidly for one minute. Keep repeating the exercise over an extended period, and eventually you will start making good progress. For example, when I used this technique when practising for my grade eight, the most time I racked up was seven hours in one day, working solely on one technique.

It sounds like a hell of a lot of time, but I really reaped the rewards. One thing you should bear in mind when you are practising in such a way is that you may not consistently be able to keep going up and up. Every so often, drop back in tempo and see how much progress you have made. For example, if you start out at 60 bpm and have spent two hours working your way to the 100 bpm end of the metronome, try dropping back to 80 bpm and see how it feels, you will amaze yourself at how this now feels 'easy' when before it would have felt impossible.

So far we have looked at good ways to use the metronome with cycled licks in order to keep pushing through your speed barriers. Inevitably you will find that you reach sticking points in your playing, where you just can't go any faster. This next idea is what I like to call a shock tactic, in order to force your fingers to move faster. This idea only really works with exercises that involve string crossing. Yet the fundamental principle can be applied to single string concepts too.

So when you reach a sticking point, where you just can't get any faster, you need to get really creative in your technical advances. One way that I've tried, is to incorporate string skips. When we play normal scalar passages on the guitar, we usually go up one string at a time. If we skip strings out, it creates a further demand on the hand, which once again will force improvement.

In Example 62 you will see an exercise in position one of the C major scale, similar to those that we saw in the legato chapter.

Example 62

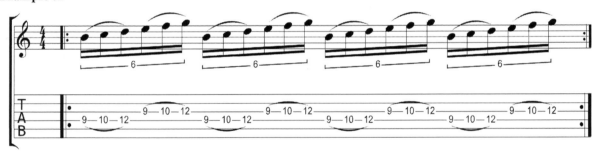

With this exercise, first you need to find out what your maximum tempo is. Using a metronome, play this exercise at gradual tempos until you find a speed where you can only play it for a few revolutions before you either lose timing or you just can't keep up. Once you have established your maximum speed for the lick, you can begin the next stage.

What I want you to do is put your metronome up around 15 to 20 bpm higher than your current maximum. This idea seems ridiculous; as you can't possibly play this speed, can you? How could you if it's that much faster than your maximum? That's why at this speed, you only want to try to accomplish two full revolutions of the lick, like in Example 63.

Example 63

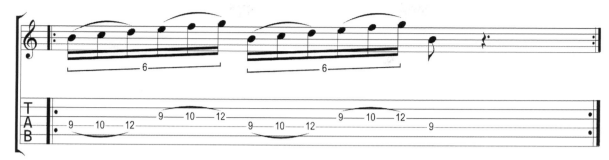

You should now be playing the exercise twice round at a tempo that far overreaches your last speed, and if you're doing it right, you should be struggling! The next phase of this idea is to add a string skip, which makes it even harder. The string I'm going to skip to is the B string, and we will be using frets eight, ten and twelve. So we will be borrowing notes from outside of position one, but this way it does sound slightly more melodic. Aim to play the exercise twice round again.

Example 64

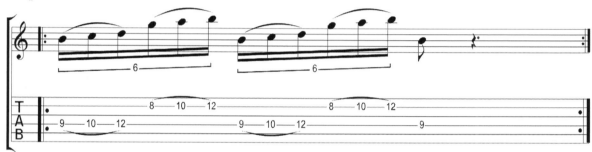

I would aim to try this idea for around five minutes before moving on to Example 65. After five minutes of this, your hand should be suffering. Make sure that when you feel pain and exhaustion in your hand, you stop for a few seconds and shake off. We want to improve our speed, strength and stamina in the hand but we don't want to be causing unnecessary injuries. Once you are just about getting comfortable with Example 64, Example 65 adds another string skip!

Example 65

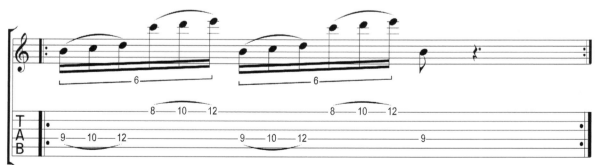

Example 65 is particularly brutal, so don't worry about the fact that you will be making lots of mistakes all over the place. Just try your absolute hardest to make that jump. Although it's going to be sounding horrible, and you won't be making this ridiculous jump, your hand is really progressing with the original lick. The next phase should feel slightly easier, as now you need to back off the metronome so that it is around 8 to 10 bpm higher than your original top speed. You also need to revert back to your first string skip, so you are only skipping one string. Now, in Example 66, what you will need to do is try to play your first string skip exercise continuously.

Example 66

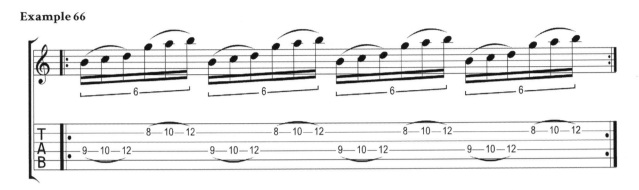

Once you have played through Example 66 for around five minutes, keep your metronome at the same speed, so that you are 8 to 10 bpm above your original top speed, and now try to play the original lick. After all of the other punishing exercises we have done, this should now feel much easier and hopefully allow you to play the original lick much faster. For single string concepts, all of the ideas in terms of metronome use will work, but obviously we can't add string skips to a single string idea. The way to make these harder is to add wider stretches. For example, you could be looking at using a single string legato idea such as Example 67.

Example 67

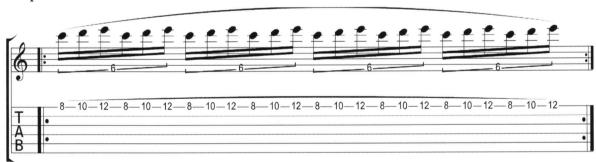

Example 67 uses a portion of our C major scale. Once you have established your top speed for this kind of idea you can make it harder by widening the stretch in certain fingers. If you move your tenth fret and twelfth fret notes along, so you fret the eleventh and fourteenth frets, you now get a fingering for a C diminished arpeggio, in much the same way that Paul Gilbert would finger one. Combine this harder fingering with the same metronome process as we used before, and you now have a lick you can use to improve a single string idea as in Example 68. Remember not to play this harder version continuously at first, give it time to bed in.

Example 68

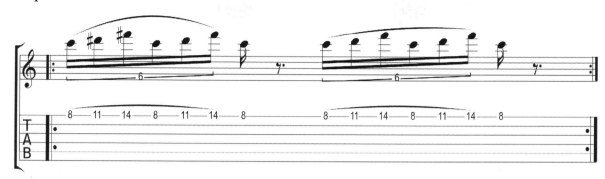

We have looked extensively at using this technique with legato ideas. It works equally well with the alternate picking technique and certain tapping examples as well. It doesn't lend itself quite so well to sweep ideas, but you can use the earlier methods perfectly well with sweep ideas to get good results.

The final idea we should look at in your quest for speed development, is the technique of rhythmic displacement. The idea here is to move the notes of licks or exercises around in terms of where they fall on the beat. What this idea does, is less about making your speeds improve but making sure you have complete command of a lick at what you believe to be your top speed. Many players push themselves on up the metronome notches when they haven't really mastered a lick at a certain tempo. The lick may still sound sloppy even if you feel you can play at a particular speed. With rhythmic displacement, you get to hear every little part of the lick and essentially iron out any creases.

We looked at using this technique in **High Intensity Guitar Technique Book One** with our sweep examples. Now we need to focus on using this idea with any type of lick in order to push forward with speed, also making sure that your licks are as fluid and clean as possible. The best time to use rhythmic displacement is when you find a sticking point in your playing. For example, you may have a lick that you just can't play any faster than 80 bpm. If this is the case, what I would do is stick at 80 bpm but use rhythmic displacement to find out if there are any problems across the lick.

The first thing you need to do when employing rhythmic displacement is to establish a top speed with a cycled lick. This can be done with any rhythmic exercise as long as the exercise is one straight rhythm. For example, if you play the lick in sixteenth notes, there will be four available displacements, but in sixteenth note triplets there will be six available displacements. We are going to use Example 18b from our legato section as a starting point. I've rewritten the example here to jog your memory.

Example 18b (from legato chapter)

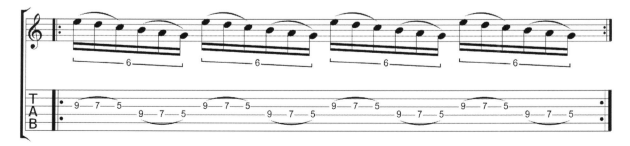

Once you have established a comfortable speed for which you can play this lick. We shall begin displacing the rhythm so that a different note falls on the downbeat of the lick (by downbeat we mean a 1, 2, 3 or 4 beat of the bar). The most obvious way to do this is to play the exercise starting and ending on what was our second note. This is shown in Example 69. Make sure you take a good listen to the Example 69 audio before diving in to the lick.

Example 69

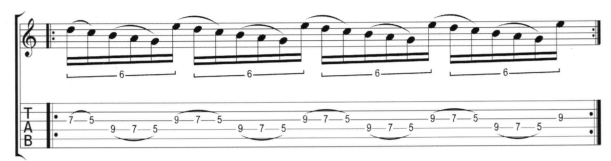

Surprisingly this version of the same lick feels much harder. It's exactly the same notes being played in the same order, and with the same fingering. Yet when the downbeat is displaced to that second note, it feels and sounds completely different. I'm sure playing the lick this way has shown you where there are weak spots in your technique. This is good. Because now you will know which part of the lick you need to fix in order to play faster. The main thing to look out for is that the timing between each note is nice and even. The obvious giveaway that you're not playing the lick right, is if the D note on your seventh fret G string is not the note falling on the downbeat each time you play the lick.

Once you are comfortable with the first displacement, check out Example 70, which shows the four remaining possibilities for displacement ideas with this exercise. When playing each one, first try to play it just once round with your metronome. That way you will get the new sound of the displacement in your ears. Once you have this, try playing it twice round comfortably before trying to play it continuously.

Usually the most difficult part to these licks is not in the mechanical motion of the fingers. It is usually due to the brain thinking that the lick sounds wrong, and therefore finding it harder as your brain naturally wants to hear the first note of the lick on the downbeat. I always found it so helpful to have each displacement ringing in my ears before trying to play it continuously.

Example 70

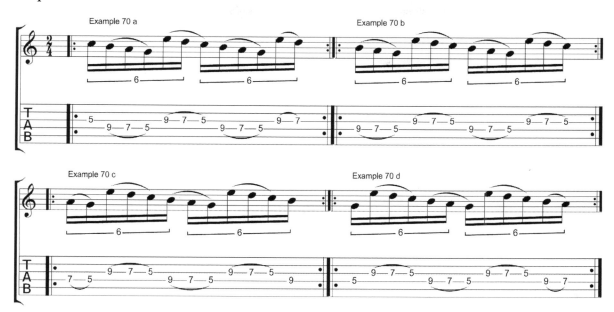

Once you have mastered the displacement ideas for the exercises presented in this chapter, the next place to start would be the ascending version of this exercise. This in itself presents a whole new world of different challenges. Once you have gotten this idea down, make sure to use rhythmic displacement on any technical work you are performing, thus making sure you have a lick as clean as you can make it.

Throughout this chapter we have looked at a number of ways to improve our speed on the guitar. Let's recap them so that we have clear in our minds the different approaches to building speed on the guitar.

Developing speed checklist:

✓ **Go up in sensible increments with a metronome.**

✓ **Try going far beyond what you are capable of to push yourself. (Shocking methods.)**

✓ **Give yourself enough time to bed in new tempos.**

✓ **Use the one minute method (going up 1 bpm a minute, rest for a minute, go again).**

✓ **Use string skips and wider stretches to make licks harder.**

✓ **Use rhythmic displacement to iron out problems across licks.**

Every technique I have talked about in this chapter has been used by me to improve certain problems in my own playing. I have also used them with countless students over the years, who have all made varying degrees of progress depending on the amount of time they invested in practising. All of these techniques are extremely useful and will yield excellent results but only if you put in plenty of effort with your technique.

If at any point you feel uninspired or despondent when playing these ideas, listen to lots of music that has great technical skill in, or watch videos of your favourite players. There is always plenty of inspiration to be found in listening to great music and watching great players. In the next chapter we will look at how to improve your bending skills. This will give you some new sounds for exiting licks and passages, and give your playing a polished and professional sound.

CHAPTER 6

Advanced String Bending and Vibrato

In the first book of this series, we looked at the foundations of how to correctly perform string bending and vibrato. In this chapter, we are going to look at how we can take this technique further in order to get many more interesting sounds out of the guitar, make the instrument come alive, and truly develop your own style with this technique. Of all the different techniques we will look at in this series, bending is the most important idea in the development of your own signature sound. Many players are famous for their ability to pick fast, play great sweep arpeggio passages or fluid legato lines. All of these players are known to have great bending techniques, and they all do it so differently.

Take a listen to a player like Yngwie Malmsteen. When he bends a string, he has this huge operatic sound to his playing. Eric Johnson has a wonderful violin like quality about his bending and vibrato. Steve Vai combines tone wide rock vibrato with Clapton's subtle hand movement ideas. Steve also uses a circular motion to get an exquisite sounding vibrato, which captures his emotion and passion for the instrument beautifully. Jimi Hendrix, David Gilmour, Brian May, Jimmy Page, Stevie Ray Vaughan and B.B. King are all so famous for having amazing sounding string bending, yet they are all such different players.

The list of amazing exponents of this technique is absolutely endless, and to get that top professional sound in your playing, you need to have a great facility for this technique. Now that we have the fundamental technique under our fingers from the exercises in Book One, let's look at some other considerations that will help your technique in this area flourish. The first one is your guitar itself. You need to have a look at the set-up of your guitar to see if it is easy enough for you to bend a string.

The first point here is that it is easier to bend lighter gauge strings. Gauge .009 strings or .010s are easy enough to bend. You can even go as low as .008s, but with this gauge you not only run the risk of a lot of string breaks but also you lose a lot in tone. The thicker the string, the better tone it will give. Personally, I use .009s on my Ibanez superstrat style guitars, and I use .010s on my Suhr. Both of these gauges feel great for me and tonally I get fantastic sounds from all of my instruments. I have used .008s in the past but found them to sound too thin. If you like a nice fat tone, you can go heavier than .010s but beware, as the heavier you go the more demands this will make on your hand.

Stevie Ray Vaughan is the most famous guitarist for using heavy gauge strings. Stevie used to use .013s on a strat with a really high action. Due to this he used to rip his fingers to shreds, which obviously is quite painful and stops you from playing. Stevie would apparently resolve this issue by supergluing his ripped calluses back to his fingertips. There is even an urban legend that he would superglue his fingers to his arm, and rip the flesh away to give his fingers fresh tips. If this is true, it's quite an extreme dedication to tone.

Aside from your string gauge, the other thing to consider is your guitar's action, which is the height of the strings from the neck of the guitar. An action that is too low causes a lot of fret buzz when you are playing, and can also cause the strings to choke out when bending, even though it does feel easier for the hand to bend with a lower action. A high action gives great tone but is very physically demanding, not just for bending but for general playing too. A high action makes bending harder as you have to push the string down more forcefully and then perform a bend.

I personally favour quite low actions on my guitars as it makes general playability easier, but that doesn't mean to say this is right. You have to set up your guitar to what feels right for you. Unless you are very comfortable with how to set up your guitar properly, the best thing to do is to find a good guitar tech that you can ask to set up your guitar how you want it. I have my guitar tech set the necks on my guitars so there is no relief (bow of the neck), with a relatively low action. The action on my guitars isn't crazily low, but it certainly is set for faster playing styles.

However, there is no string choking or buzzing because he has set them perfectly to allow the strings to ring at just the right height so I get maximum playability without sacrificing tone. I also quite like the necks on my guitars to feel quite flat, as this helps with fast scalar passages and also helps with bending. If you have a rounded guitar neck the strings have more chance of choking when bending. Another thing to consider is the type of frets you have on your guitar. As your frets wear down through playing, they can feel very gritty and jagged when bending. If you are experiencing this, you perhaps need a re-fret on your guitars or at least a fret dress, to get them nicely rounded again. I recommend stainless steel jumbo frets, as they last a lot longer than nickel frets and also they are high, allowing bends to be executed easier.

Once you have looked into the set-up of your guitar and are happy with the action, string gauges and the set of the neck, it's time for some physical considerations. The first are your calluses. Calluses will develop as part of your guitar playing. Just from having your hands playing through the notes over and again your calluses develop, but when bending they get severely tested. Your fingertips need to be in tip-top shape to be able to perform bends; otherwise you will experience pain that is quite detrimental to your playing.

You also need your calluses to get a good purchase on the string. Without them we can't grip so well, so when we bend, you can often lose the string, which sounds like a blatant mistake as the string pings back down to its original pitch. When you bend you want to aim to fret, bang in the middle of the calluses on your fingertips, as this gives not only the best tone but also the least chance of mistakes and dead notes. When looking at the bending examples in this chapter it is extremely important that you get your muting right. In the examples from Book One; we were performing very simple up and down bends, which is a lot easier to mute. As the bends in this chapter are a lot more involved, you will need to find many more ways of muting.

You can often use right hand palm muting as we have discussed in Book One, but as your left hand is in a completely different position with the thumb over the top of the neck, you will lose a lot of its ability to mute. When I perform bends and vibrato, I quite often hook my pick underneath the string above the one I am bending, and pull that string out of the way. I also use a spare finger from my fretting hand to lie across adjacent strings if I possibly can, to keep them quiet. When performing these ideas your hands will actively look to find ways to mute, as you will want to eradicate unwanted string noise. Go with what works for you and perfect what feels natural, after all we are trying to develop your unique style here.

Before diving in to the examples of this chapter you may wish to revisit Book One for the details on exactly how to perform bends. Make sure you remember that the hand position now has to change, so your hand is set up with the thumb over the top of the neck. Remember too that it's really important that the fingers alone don't do the bending. Bends should also come from a good turn in the wrist like a key turning a lock on a door.

The final point to remember is that wherever possible, you need to support the finger performing a bend with others. If you can avoid it, you don't want to be bending with just one finger for tone wide singing bends. Sometimes it is necessary to bend with one finger depending on how you exit a lick, and of course for microtonal blues bends and vibrato purposes, the first finger alone can perform bends. But wherever possible, when bending, use at least two fingers from your fretting hand.

Once you're happy with how to perform bends from the Book One examples, take a look at the first of the examples in this chapter. The bending examples in this book are the building blocks for licks that you can use in your own solos, improvisation and as exit points for your runs and soloing ideas.

Example 71 is a bluesy based idea in the style of Jimi Hendrix. You're going to be moving through different pentatonic positions whilst incorporating bends as a part of scalar passages. You need to be careful here of your hand positioning, as it is hard to perform the bend and then get back into a position where you can perform the scalar parts.

Example 71

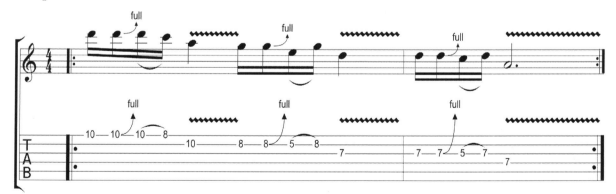

Example 72 is a common blues-rock idea. You're playing a repeating lick incorporating a second string bend followed by some hammer-ons and pull-offs. The exit point is a tone wide bend on the second string, which would be held with added vibrato. This kind of idea can be found all over the playing of blues, rock and metal guitar players. For an excellent example of how this sort of thing can work in context, I would recommend checking out Joe Satriani's entrance to the *G3: Live in Denver* DVD. Joe uses loads of this sort of technique during the intro solo to his set. In fact, check out the whole concert! There is awesome playing galore on that DVD.

Example 72

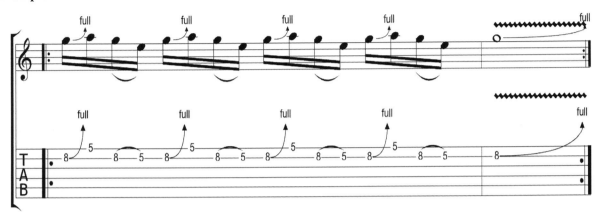

Example 73 uses a technique made famous by Blues guitarist Albert king. This is the technique of the over bend. When you over bend, you push a note beyond the usual tone width. You can go as far as you feel appropriate to capture the emotion and sound you wish; this idea is all about making the guitar scream. Usually an over bend is a tone and a half in width. From a scalar point of view, sometimes the next pentatonic note is a tone and a half away, so over bends allow you to bend in less common areas of the scale. For these big bends you will need to make sure you have a tight grip on the string, otherwise you won't make the bend up to full pitch. Players like Stevie Ray Vaughan and David Gilmour are also famed for their use of wide over bends.

Example 73

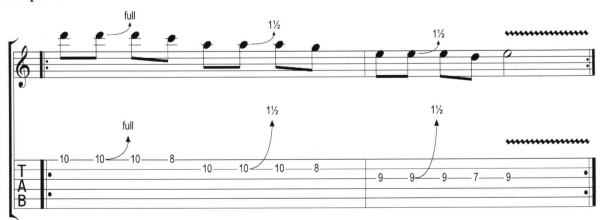

Example 74 is a bend idea that needs to be in the vocabulary of every guitarist. It's been so overplayed that not only do you need it in your improvisational playing to sound like a guitarist, but if you are serious about soloing and learning other people's solos, you're going to come across this lick quite a lot. What you need to do is bend the seventh fret on your third string in the usual fashion, but leave your first finger spare. Once you have performed the bend, your first finger will lie flat across the fifth fret on strings one and two, and play the notes one after the other. Use your choice of alternate or economy style picking for this. Once you have played the lick once, you then repeat it to your heart's content.

Example 74

Example 75 is another common blues and rock based idea. We are keeping the lick from Example 74 but now we are going to add a pull-off on the second string from the eighth fret to the fifth fret. This kind of idea can be found all over the playing of guitarists, right from Hendrix, to Kirk Hammett, Joe Bonamassa or Satriani. This sort of idea also works slowly, fast, with bluesy break-up from your amp or with huge distortion. It's just a great guitar lick that works in many stylistic situations. Try incorporating this sort of thing into your solos right away. The exit point I have used is to play the seventh fret third string, tone wide bend with added vibrato, but feel free to come up with your own exit to the lick.

Example 75

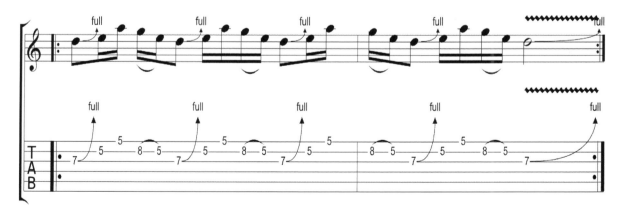

Example 76 is more of an exercise than lick based, but you will easily be able to incorporate this idea into solos to great effect. The idea here is to play a full tone bend at the eighth fret on your second string, but really slowly. This is hard to do, and will train your ability to control your bends from a technical perspective. It will also train your ear as you will be able to hear many more microtonal pitches this way. Once you have a good control over your bends, you will be able to vary the speed of bends in solos to give different textures to your playing. When bending, it creates a tension if you can slowly raise the note to pitch rather than playing directly to the desired pitch. There are times when both ways are necessary in your solos, but being able to vary the way you play your bends will allow you to add more emotion and character to solos.

Example 76

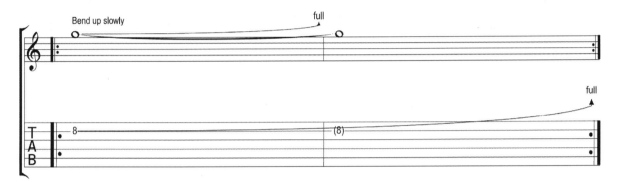

Example 77 is an idea based around the D Dorian mode. The Dorian mode is a seven note scale and is the second mode of the major scale. In this particular case, the D Dorian mode is the second mode in the key of C major, which means we don't need to learn any new scale shapes in order to be able to play the scale. The easiest way to visualize this lick, is that you are using the D minor pentatonic scale in position one, with an added ninth and an added sixth interval. What we are looking at here is how to employ a half bend, to reach notes that are only a semitone away, rather than a full tone away.

When you perform a half bend, the technique is exactly the same as tone bends, except you exert less force so that the note will only be raised a semitone in pitch. This idea works really well with modal based licks, as there are many places in these scales where you can bend up a semitone to reach the next note of the scale. Take a listen to players like Robben Ford and Larry Carlton to hear how these melodic and tasteful type players use this idea.

Example 77

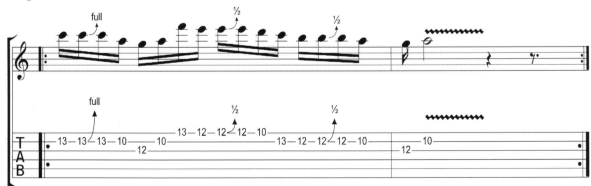

Example 78 is another idea based on Robben Ford's playing. Robben is one of the tastiest players out there today, and is famous for his jazzy influenced blues guitar playing. This lick is commonly found in his standard pentatonic bluesy approach. What you want to aim for here is a nice controlled sound of the lick. Rhythmically this lick is played quite straight and all of the notes sounding like they seamlessly blend from one to another. Make sure your bends are reaching a nice full, singing quality and for the exit add a smooth vibrato rather than an aggressive, metal style vibrato. Check out Robben's solo on the song 'Badge', which he covers on the *Keep On Running* album to listen to lots of this sort of playing. His song 'How Deep in the Blues' from the album *Truth* also has loads of great licks.

Example 78

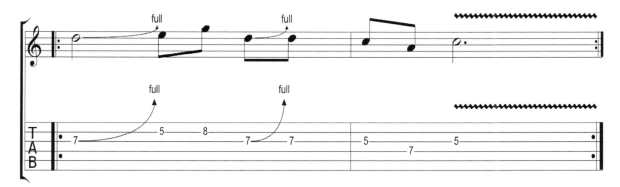

Example 79 is a very demanding idea as we have quite a mix of full tone bends, pre-bends, and released bends all in one lick. First you perform the common blues-rock idea from Example 74. You exit this to a full tone bend on the eighth fret second string. Once you have bent that note to full pitch, you then need to hold that bend and leave it ringing. Whilst that is ringing out, you then use your fourth finger underneath it to play the eighth fret on the first string, so that both these notes ring at the same time.

The second string note may start to ring off as it will have been up at pitch for quite some time. This is OK though as we will now re-pick it anyway, and treat it as a pre-bent note. So pick that note and whilst ringing let it down to its original, unbent pitch. Once you have done this we then begin a new idea starting at the fifth fret on the second string. The second bar of this exercise is a very common bluesy idea. There is a lot to get through in this lick, but if you can manage to mix up your bends like this you will start to get a wonderful singing quality about your playing.

Example 79

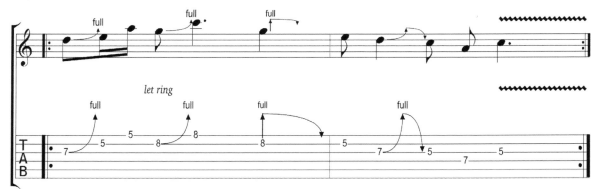

Example 80 is another idea incorporating half bends. In this example, we are looking at how players add intervals such as the ninth to minor pentatonic soloing to add a sophisticated and classy touch. This sort of thing is reminiscent of bands such as Thin Lizzy, who like to hint at modes when playing pentatonic runs. Once again Larry Carlton is great at this kind of thing. Check out players like Steve Lukather or Dann Huff to hear how great session players add this kind of thing to pop and rock solos.

Example 80

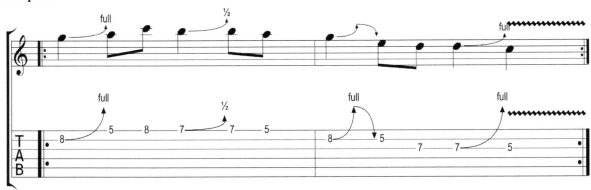

Example 81 is all about microtonal bends. Any of you familiar with the blues probably already use microtonal bends naturally in most of your playing. If you are a really keen blues player, they get so ingrained into your playing that it's hard not to add them to almost anything you're playing, but you do need to be aware that they aren't always stylistically appropriate. A microtonal bend is often known as a quarter tone bend, and that is how they will be shown in the notation. We know that when we play a full bend, we go up a tone in pitch, and a half bend is a semitone in pitch. A microtonal bend is not really a proper note, but is somewhere between a half bend and an unbent note. If you are bending the eighth fret on your high E string microtonally, you would be playing a pitch somewhere between C and C#.

This idea is used extensively by blues and rock guitarists to add a gritty character to soloing. Once you are familiar with this sound, you will find it hard to play notes without doing it, as it just sounds so cool. Technically these bends are performed in much the same way as any other bend but the motion is only very small. You need to develop the link between your ears and your fingers so you can feel and hear the desired pitch when you're playing. Example 81 shows how this sort of thing can be done in the standard 'box one' of A minor pentatonic. Make sure to get comfortable doing this all over the neck.

Example 81

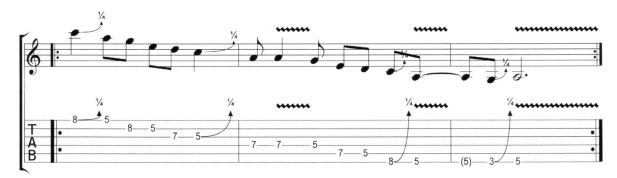

Example 82 is the last string bending example we shall look at before taking a close look at vibrato. This example is all about developing the maximum amount of control you can possibly get out of bends. The idea here is to be able to play four consecutive chromatic notes starting at the eighth fret second string, up and down, all with bends. If you can do this, you really do have great control of your bending technique.

Essentially, you will perform a half bend, a full bend, and then a tone and a half over bend on the way up. Then you will release these bends back down, so in essence playing a pre-bent tone and a half over bend. This is released to a tone bend, then to a half bend and back to the original pitch. Playing the bends in this way will mean you are ascending and descending four notes chromatically. This is extremely hard to do but if you can perform this idea correctly, you have pretty much mastered the technique of string bending.

Example 82

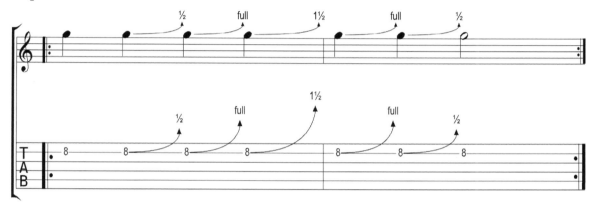

Example 82 concludes the string bending examples for this chapter. Hopefully these examples will provide a platform for you to be able to come up with your own ideas on how to use this technique. As always, once you've practised it well and feel capable with the technique, start using it in your solos and improvisation.

Now let's take a look at a new way of practising the vibrato technique. In my opinion, vibrato is a very much overlooked technique by players, in the sense that guitarists don't practise it in the same way that they would other techniques. For example, not enough guitarists sit down and practise vibrato exercises. This begs the question of, why not?

A good vibrato is one of the most important parts in a player's identity. It not only helps you to sound, well, like you, but it is one of the most important aspects of getting a polished and professional sound. In essence, you need your vibrato to sound great, as if it doesn't, nobody will care how fast you can play or how awesome your latest sweep arpeggio sounds. If your exit points to your licks sound awful then all you will be remembered for is that terrible tone. In Example 83 I have outlined an exercise that I came up with in order to be able to practise my vibrato on all four fingers, and on different strings. Firstly, vibrato needs to be practised on all four fingers so that no matter what kind of lick you are playing, you will be comfortable in the knowledge that whatever fingers you exit your lick on, you can exit the lick with a great tone.

The reason vibrato needs to be practised on all strings, is because every string has a different tension, meaning the amount of force required to vibrato a note will feel different. Also, different strings require different directions of vibrato, much like string bending. If you are using vibrato on the sixth, fifth, fourth or third string then your vibrato needs to move in a downwards fashion. Whilst using vibrato on the first and second string you will use a push-up motion.

In Example 83, the idea is to play up four notes of a three notes per string scale form. Then you will come back to the second note of that scale shape, and whatever finger lands on that note, use vibrato for two beats until moving through the scale again. What you do now is ascend through another four notes, then back two, and vibrato that note again. It's a bit like playing through a scale sequence where you stop to vibrato certain notes of that sequence.

As you play through the example, you will notice that at some point, every finger has landed on the note to be played with vibrato, so this is a great way to practise your vibrato. When using this idea, make sure to play to a metronome or drum machine. What you should hear rhythmically, if you want a wide vibrato, is 1 + 2 + 3 pulse, pulse, pulse. That way your vibrato will be nicely in time to the music. Take a good listen to the audio demonstration to hear how I play this vibrato.

You may of course want a shallower, faster vibrato than I have used. That is absolutely fine as you creating the sound in your head is the most important thing. I would still urge you to practise this technique to a timekeeping device and also aim to keep your vibrato in time to the music that you are playing. Whether it is fast, wide, shallow or slow, your vibrato will sound much sweeter if it pulses in time to the music you are playing. When playing Example 83, make sure you are using the correct fingerings for three notes per string, as that way you will make sure you get the most even distribution of vibrato on different fingers. Also, make sure to try this idea with all seven three notes per string shapes, try it in descending fashion too for different approaches and, obviously, in different keys.

Example 83

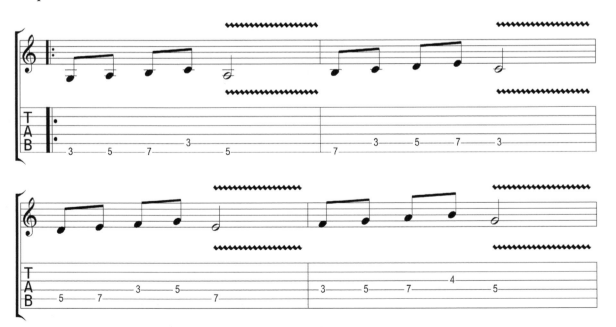

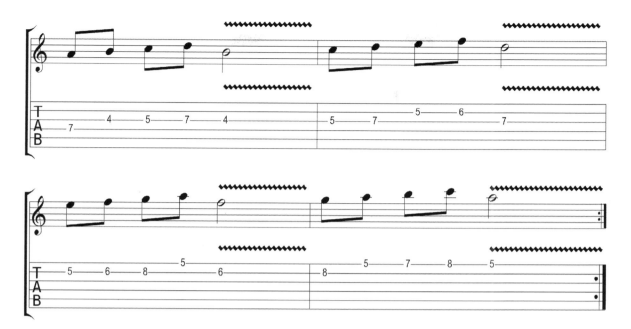

In this chapter, you have learned lots of new ways to expand your technical ability with the string bending and vibrato techniques. Make sure that you have spent lots of time getting this technique completely mastered, as I can't stress enough how important it is to getting a good sound to your playing. You will also need your bending to be as sharp as possible to make good use of the next chapter.

In the next chapter, we will be looking at how to turn the ideas we have previously learned in the book into actual licks. These can then be used in your own composed solos, or your improvisation, in order for you to start soloing in a professional lead guitar role.

Chapter 7

Licks and Musical Phrases

In Book One of this series and in the previous chapters of this second book, we have looked at lots of different mechanical exercises. These ideas are all excellent for developing your technique in many areas of guitar 'playing', yet they don't necessarily create good 'music'. This chapter is all about taking the mechanical ideas adhered to so far, and making them into a musical idea that can be used in your compositions, or your improvised solos.

Most of the examples we have looked at so far in Book One and Two make up the nucleus of some great guitar licks. Many of you I'm sure will have played through certain examples and said, 'Ah, I see, that sounds like the sort of thing Jimmy Page would do,' or Hendrix, or Brian May, Steve Vai etc.

The thing is, for a repeated exercise to really sound like a lick that one of these great players may use, we need to lead into it with some kind of melodious musical phrase, then play our awesome technical chops, and finally exit with an expressive and emotive outro to the phrase. Essentially, to get these exercises to sound more musical, they need to be sandwiched between other musical ideas.

The next question to answer is probably: so what is a guitar lick anyway?

This is a very important question, as without knowing the answer, it's hard to know the difference between mindless noodling of notes and trying to create music that moves people. The first thing to be aware of is that a lick is very different to a riff. A riff, by definition, is a repeating pattern within a song. When associated with contemporary guitar playing, a riff can either be played with chords of all types (especially power chords in rock and metal genres) or single notes, usually in the bass end of the neck, for creating the rhythm guitar part.

Licks are mainly associated with lead guitar. They can also be played in the bass part of the neck but are usually for soloing concepts rather than for rhythm concepts. A lick mainly consists of single note melodic lines, but can include double stops and triads etc. Licks form the basis of composed guitar solos, which are usually supplemented with runs that players use to get from one lick to another, and are heavily drawn upon during improvisation.

Jazz, blues and rock guitarists are well known to have favourite licks that they draw upon to create their own personal style. Many players create lick banks, or compilations of their favourite licks in notation and tab so they can refer to them for inspiration when soloing. Before you can start developing your own unique style and licks, it's definitely a good idea to learn lots of licks from your favourite players.

The best way to do this, as I outlined in the beginning of Book One, is to transcribe. If you have a particular guitarist that you really like, listening to lots of his or her playing and working out the source of their licks is a great way to do so. This way you develop your ear, so you can more easily recreate licks that sound similar yourself when improvising.

Now we know what a lick is, we can begin getting into the correct mindset for learning the licks in this chapter. There are twenty licks, composed mainly using the guitarist's favourite pentatonic scale. There are certain passages incorporating arpeggio and three notes per string ideas in these licks, but once you have these 'common approach' licks under your fingers, we will discuss in the continued development chapter how to further enhance other ideas, like your three notes per string playing.

The licks combine all of the technical elements we have looked at in these two books. They are also composed in different genres, so you can see how each technique can be applied in different ways to get great effects in different styles. In the interest of being a more rounded player, you don't want to get boxed in as just a rock, or just a jazz guitar player. To reach the most professional levels of musicianship, and make yourself more employable (if that is your goal with the guitar), you need to have a good handle on all genres, as the more you can play, the more likely you are to be out there, playing.

If, however, you are just playing the guitar for fun, it's still a great idea to play in as many styles as possible, as if you're a rocker, having some tasty blues licks or having the harmonic quality of jazz about your playing can only help your rock chops get better. Take guitar legend Steve Lukather. He has got some great blues licks in his playing and is quite capable of using all the harmonically interesting lines found in jazz. This gives him a nice fusion style quality to his rock chops. Check out any live footage of him playing with the band Toto to hear his sophisticated style.

On the accompanying download I have demonstrated each lick slow and fast so that you can hear how each one should sound. Each lick is demonstrated over a relevant chord, so that you can hear each lick in some context. Certain licks will be demonstrated over a static chord, like A minor 7, which you will see notated above the lick just as Am7. Other licks will be demonstrated over a progression, and you will see each chord above the music where it is played.

At the end of the book I have also included seven full jam tracks, including two blues backings, and one of each of the following styles: rock, funk, fusion, jazz and metal. You can use these tracks to create your own licks and practise jamming over them. The jam tracks and how to play over them will be outlined later. For now, let's get our teeth into these licks.

Our first lick, shown in Example 84, is a rapid fire modern rock lick in the style of great guitarists such as Eddie Van Halen and Randy Rhoads. On the bulk of the lick, for the hammered and pulled notes, use whichever fingering you feel most comfortable with. A combination of either fingers 1, 4, 1, 3 or 1, 3, 1, 2 are recommended. On the exit, use your third finger for the tone wide bends, and use a tone wide rock vibrato exit for stylistic accuracy.

Example 84

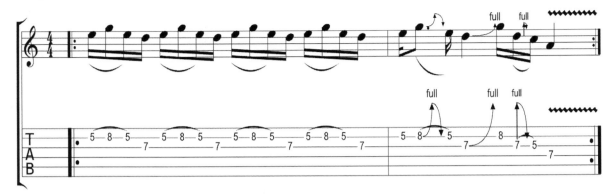

Our second lick is another from the rock genre, and is in the style of greats such as Ritchie Blackmore from Deep Purple and the Scorpions legend Uli Jon Roth. Both of these guitarists were instrumental in pushing the heavy metal genre forward with melodic and neoclassical soloing. Example 85 captures how they incorporated standard blues licks into their flashier rock style with the use of fast pull-offs.

Use the standard third finger for the tone wide bends, but use your fourth finger for the pull-offs on the top two strings. This will make your third fingers workload a little less tiring during the lick. Exit to the seventh fret on the fourth string (the root note of our minor pentatonic scale) with either a wide, slow style rock vibrato, or a shallow and fast rock style vibrato.

Example 85

Example 86 is a modern rock sequence idea in the style of Paul Gilbert. The lick starts with an ascending run in position one of A minor pentatonic, incorporating lots of left hand pull-offs, similar to the kind of pentatonic playing Paul used in his heyday with Mr Big. The exit to the run incorporates full and half bends. Many rock players, including Paul, like to manipulate bends to give them a very dirty, gritty edge to them. Sometimes, it's even OK to bend slightly out of key if this evokes the feel you are looking for in your solo. Once you've played the bends, the outro to the lick is a descending run incorporating the flattened fifth from the blues scale.

Use a mix of alternate picking and legato to execute this part, making sure to use fingers 1, 3 and 4 on the three notes per string section as Paul would. The final exit note of the lick is the fifth fret on the third string, which is incidentally the minor third interval of the scale. This is a common place to exit your licks when you are bored of hearing the 'safe' root note. Again use tone wide rock vibrato for stylistic accuracy.

Example 86

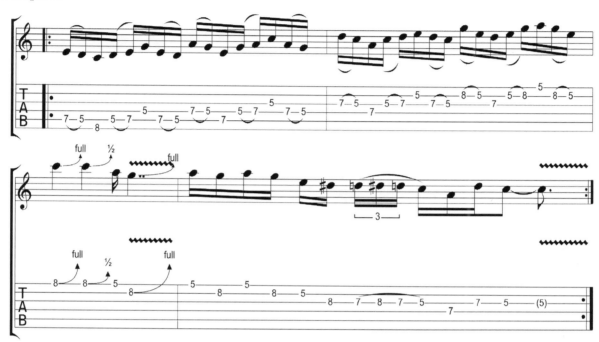

Example 87 is another rock lick in the style of melodic rocker Andy Timmons. Andy is a great player, and is as comfortable playing blisteringly fast as he is playing a really emotive and soulful melody. In this lick, we are looking at his ability to capture a soulful mood by using the over bending technique and adding upper extension notes to pentatonic playing. The lick starts with a common rock and blues bending lick in A minor pentatonic position one, then we employ the over bending technique at the tenth fret on the B string.

This means we first bend up from the root note to the ninth interval relative to A (a B note) and then bend again to a C with the over bend, the C being the minor third, so we've outlined a nice minor ninth sound in the lick. In the second bar use either alternate or sweep picking to play the ascending A minor arpeggio, which exits to frets thirteen, and ten (notes F and D), which are the thirteenth and eleventh upper extension tones of A.

In bar three, we exit the lick with another hint at the ninth interval before holding the A root at the tenth fret. Make sure to use your vibrato in as expressive a manner as you can with this lick. If you really like these sounds, try adding in the upper extension tones to your own pentatonic playing. You can get some really exotic and modal flavours with this idea, without needing to learn tons of shapes; you just need knowledge of the intervals relative to your root note.

Example 87

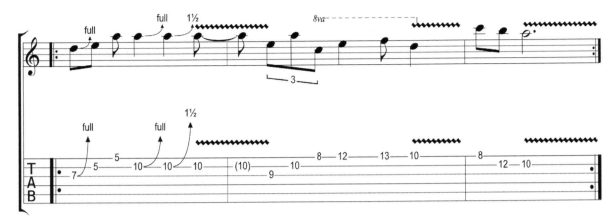

Our next lick shown in Example 88, is a cascading sextuplet idea in the style of Eric Johnson. Once again this lick is purely pentatonic, but uses shapes five, four and three all in one go. Firstly, we start in position four with a little lead in to the bulk of the lick. Then we play a sextuplet pattern in position five that moves its way through position four and finally, stopping on the minor third in position four for a beat.

This gives us just enough time to catch our breath before we begin descending through the third position, once again in sextuplets. The exit to the lick is a nice little slide effect from the root, in to the minor third and back to the root. As this is predominantly a legato lick, it sounds nice to incorporate the slide at the end rather than have the more common bends, and adds a slightly different flavour than using more hammers and pulls.

Example 88

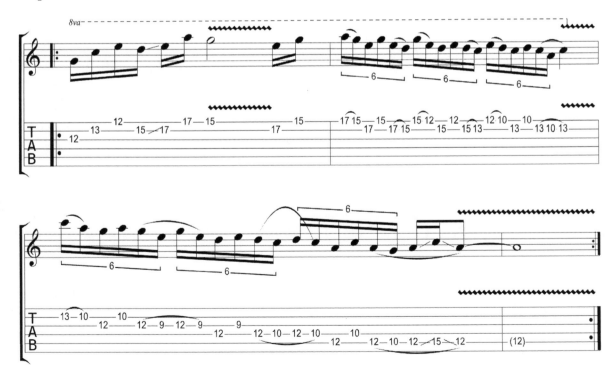

Example 89 is a fusion lick, inspired by guitarists such as Greg Howe and Richie Kotzen. The lick uses a combination of legato and economy picking throughout, both of which are techniques very popular among the fusion style guitarists. The lick is being executed in a combination of E minor and A minor pentatonic. Fusion players like to mix and match their pentatonic scales to pull out exotic flavours of modes. In this case we are playing E minor pentatonic over an A minor backing, which outlines nicely an Am11 sound. The opening to the lick is a repeated legato idea that will require your fretting hand to be moving around on the first string whilst playing a static idea on the second string.

Make sure to use a barre of the third finger to play the two notes at the fifteenth fret. Use a fingering of 1, 3 and 4 throughout this part of the lick. The outro to the lick is a descending run in A minor pentatonic position four incorporating economy picking. Economy picking keeps with the smooth sounding approach from the previous legato idea. To hear loads of these types of licks in action, check out the two albums Greg Howe and Richie Kotzen did together titled *Project* and *Tilt*.

Example 89

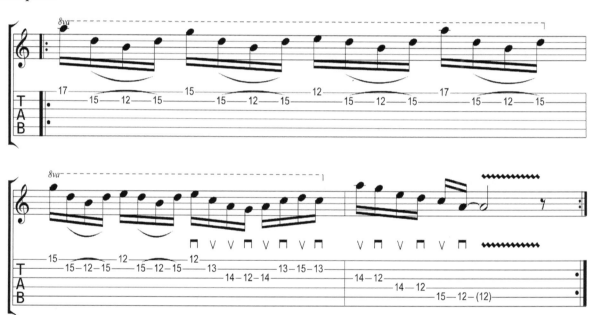

Example 90 is a lick that combines bluesy phrasing followed by fast and aggressive sounding picked runs. In modern rock and fusion genres, players quite often use blues based pentatonic ideas for their phrasing followed by fast runs using three notes per string modal scales. Check out players such as John Petrucci from Dream Theater, who is a master of this kind of soloing idea.

In this particular lick we are playing a bending idea based in position four of A minor pentatonic, followed by a sixteenth note descending run in the A natural minor scale. I have left out pick directions from the lick, as you should try this with both alternate and economy picking to see not only which you favour, but which you are best at. That way you will know which of the two techniques to prioritise in your practice.

Example 90

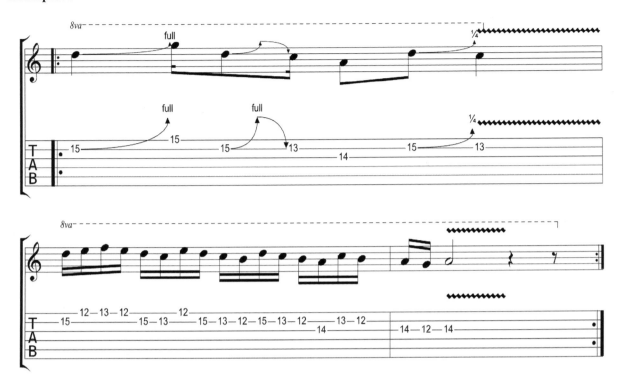

Example 91 is a sweep picking lick, incorporating several different arpeggios. Players such as Jason Becker from the rock genre use this idea, and Frank Gambale uses these ideas in his jazz and fusion playing. Normally when playing through fast arpeggio passages players tend to play one key, and play different inversions of that same arpeggio along the neck. In this lick we are playing four different keys of arpeggio along the neck.

The reason for this, is that when you extract arpeggios that are diatonic (belong to one key), you can hear extension notes that outline the sound of a mode (larger scales). If you play the same triad but in different inversions, all you hear is the same three notes all of the time. Using different arpeggios to pull out certain tones of a mode is a very sophisticated way to use the sweeping idea and will bring much more harmonic interest to your solos.

Firstly, in Example 91, we play a C major arpeggio, followed by an E minor 7 arpeggio, a G major arpeggio and finally finishing on a B minor 7 arpeggio. When we superimpose these arpeggios over the A minor backing, we get a really cool fusion sound that is as at home with jazz as it is in making for sophisticated rock licks. The run on the end of the arpeggios is just a descending A natural minor scale which exits with a tone wide, first finger pull down bend.

Example 91

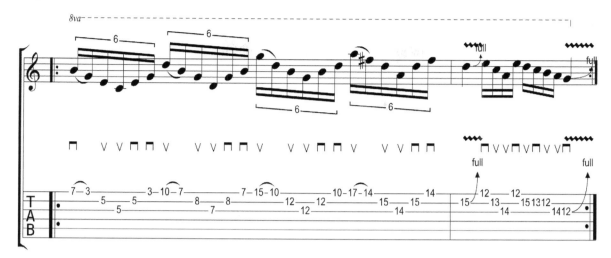

Example 92 is a lick that incorporates the legato and tapping technique, very much in the style of Eddie Van Halen. When he burst on to the scene in the late '70s he completely revolutionized the way we play the electric guitar. His fast and fluid legato runs, alternate picked lines and, of course, his blistering tapping technique literally blew his audiences away.

In this lick, we begin using the common third string bend with double stop blues rock idea, exiting to a tone wide bend on the second string with wide rock vibrato. We then begin a sixteenth note legato run based around the A Dorian mode, which is a scale that adds the ninth degree and sixth degree relative to A, on top of the usual pentatonic notes. Make sure to use either fingers 1, 3 and 4 or 1, 2 and 3 to perform this part of the lick.

In bar two, we begin a descending run with a hybrid of the blues scale and Dorian mode. Van Halen and Paul Gilbert are both fans of this hybrid scale approach, referred to simply as the blues/Dorian scale. In your fretting hand you will perform a standard legato idea at frets five, seven and eight, and then tap at the twelfth fret. From here you will pull-off back down the scale, before starting the next string with a fretting hand tap, otherwise known as a 'hammer-on from nowhere'.

The idea here is to hammer your eighth fret second string with the fourth finger, tap at the twelfth fret and then descend that string. You will again repeat this process for the third string, before exiting the lick in bar three with a common rock exit idea, incorporating a first finger downwards tone bend on the minor third, and of course tone wide vibrato to finish. Check out Van Halen's song 'Hot For teacher', which has a similar lick to Example 92 in its intro. Also, for the blues/Dorian approach, check out Paul Gilbert's instructional masterpiece *Terrifying Guitar Trip* for his insight into the use of such licks.

Example 92

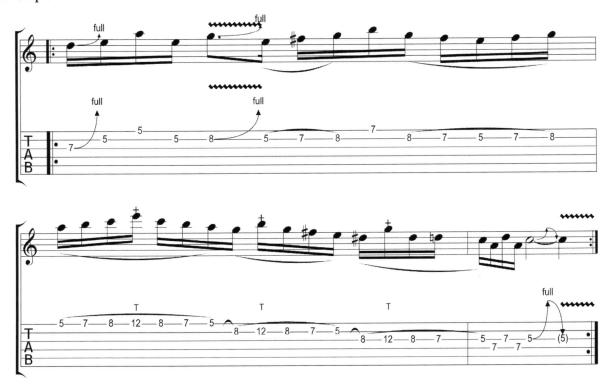

Example 93 is another tapping lick, showing you how you can move licks along the length of the neck. This lick also incorporates taps to bent notes so you can see another approach rather than just flashy fast licks. The lick begins with a run that spans four of the five shapes of A minor pentatonic. You are performing a standard hammer-on and pull-off lick, in which we will also incorporate a tapped note to get an ultra fast sounding lick. Firstly, you play the eighth fret on the first string with a tap, which you pull-off to the fifth fret on the first string. This is then followed by a fretting hand hammer-on to the eighth fret. You repeat this lick in this position one of A minor pentatonic, before sliding the whole idea up to position two and repeating. This will be performed in the same way for positions three and four respectively.

Once the four positions are completed with the initial tapping idea, we exit this part of the lick with a tone wide bend on the first string at the fifteenth fret. From here we begin a rundown through position three, which I have included the fingering for in the notation. It's very important that you use the correct fingers here to get you into the right position for the bend that follows. You should end up at the seventh fret on the third string with your third finger, so you can perform a tone wide bend with the strongest fingering.

Whilst holding the bend, you now need to tap at the twelfth fret, pulling off to the bent note and again tap at the tenth fret. The exit to the lick is a release to the minor third and then finally to play the root note (A) at the seventh fret on the D string. This kind of application is extremely popular with rock fusion artists. The lick is particularly reminiscent of Greg Howe's playing, his album *Introspection* is a must for anyone that likes this approach.

Example 93

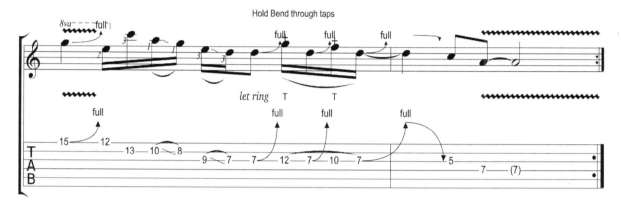

Example 94 is a pentatonic lick in the style of great blues player Robben Ford, who is well known for his exceptional phrasing and ability to play the coolest sounding licks. In Example 94 we are highlighting this ability by looking at the subtleties in Robben's bending and vibrato on the right notes, to give his standard pentatonic ideas a really sweet sound.

We begin the lick with a common ascending minor pentatonic idea in position four, in which we bend the fourth degree of the scale (the note D, found at fret fifteen, B string) up to reach the fifth degree. The fifth is an extremely strong interval to bend up to, and is the next best note to play after the root. Whilst the bend is up, we also play the flattened seventh degree on the high E string with the fourth finger, and allow those two notes to ring simultaneously.

The first bar of the lick ends with more common blues phrasing around the position four area with an exit to the minor third degree, found at the thirteenth fret on the B string. On this note, aim for a sweet sounding, subtle vibrato rather than an aggressive and wide one to get the Robben Ford sound. Lastly in bar two, we have a nice little descending run through the minor pentatonic that incorporates a first finger half bend at the thirteenth fret B string.

Incidentally, as this note is the minor third, when we bend it a half step, the note becomes the major third. This is how players such as Robben Ford get a major/minor hybrid effect in their playing. These sort of licks work perfectly over dominant 7 chords in the blues, as the chord itself has a major/minor quality about it.

Robben Ford is a master at mixing major and minor pentatonic scales, and a lot of this sound can be found just by manipulating the minor third in the scale to sound like a major third. Check out Robben's famous album *Talk to Your Daughter* to hear loads of amazing blues guitar soloing and wonderful phrasing.

Example 94

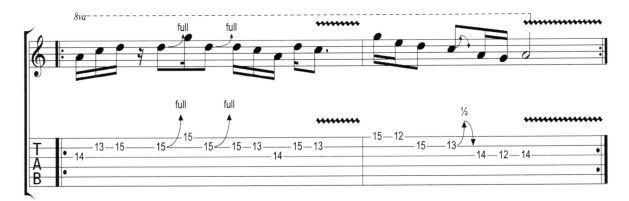

Example 95 is another blues lick that shows how the alternate picking technique can be used to get great sixteenth note style runs. This lick begins once again with a common blues bending idea. The initial bend is a slow bend up and release back down to the original pitch. We then exit with some standard blues pentatonic phrasing with an exit to the minor third with added vibrato.

In bar two, we begin a descending sixteenth note run, which utilizes the flattened fifth of the blues scale. We will then shift into position five of the minor pentatonic, and go from playing the minor third to playing the major third of the scale. For some reason, when we want to mix up the major and minor third, it sounds far more pleasing to the ear to go from the minor third to the major third than the other way round.

Due to this being the more musical way to play these two notes, we tend to play them in this order, rather than just moving chromatically down from the fifth as you may expect this lick to be played. The exit finishes on the minor third in the fifth position of the A minor pentatonic. To get this lick to sound as smooth as possible use alternate picking to get the sixteenth note pulse. Steve Morse uses lots of sixteenth note runs in his blues playing, check out his video *Power Lines* for a great insight into his playing.

Example 95

Example 96 shows another blues type lick that breaks out of the boxes and will be a good workout for your economy or alternate picking. A common problem among guitarists is that they feel 'boxed in' to one pentatonic or blues scale shape, and find it hard to utilize the full length of the neck. Later on we are going to look at a few licks that span the full fretboard, but in this lick we are going to use three of our minor pentatonic forms.

In bar one, the lick begins with an ascending run using the technique of mixing the major and minor third. Add a touch of subtle vibrato on the exit root note of this bar. As we move into bar two we are playing a descending run in position three of the scale. Watch out for the tricky triplet rhythms on this run. Finally, in bar three we play an ascending position four idea that exits on the root of the scale with subtle bluesy vibrato. Try combining pentatonic forms in this manner to create your own licks that 'break out' of the boxes.

Example 96

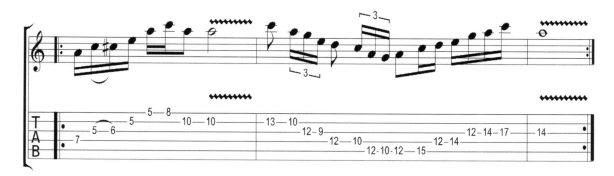

Example 97 is a fusion style lick, based very much on the playing of guitarists such as Frank Gambale and Scott Henderson. The lick is being played over a Dm7 backing and is based on two concepts. Firstly, the economy picking technique is the way forward in executing the lick. The second concept to get your head around is the art of pentatonic substitution, which is being used in this lick.

The lick starts with a run in the D Dorian mode (second mode of C major). This is a three notes per string idea and will be fairly straight forward to learn from following the tab example. In bars two and three, we begin descending runs in the E minor, D minor and A minor pentatonic scales. The reason this works, is because all three of those minor pentatonic scales live inside the C major scale and all of its modes.

If this is a sound you like, remember that whatever chord you are playing over from within a major scale, there are always three different minor pentatonic scales that will work over it. The way to work this out, is to go back to the parent key of the chord, and build a pentatonic scale on each of the three minor chords that live in that key. For more help with this kind of idea, check out some music theory about harmonizing scales.

Example 97

Example 98 is another fusion style lick using similar methods to Example 97. This time we are going for a smoother legato sound and are going to be ascending scale forms in sextuplets, so the lick is very technically demanding. The lick begins with an economy picked descending Dm7 arpeggio in sixteenth notes. We then move in to an ascending D minor pentatonic lick in position five, which we then shift along to position one. The backing for the lick is in D minor, so the scale is the same as the chord in the backing.

The next thing we do though is begin ascending the E minor pentatonic scale in the same technical fashion. This scale gives us the root, fifth, ninth, eleventh and thirteenth intervals relative to D, so we get all of the upper extension tones of D by superimposing this scale. We then follow suit with A minor pentatonic over D, which gives us the root, fifth, flat seventh, ninth and eleventh relative to D, so it outlines a Dm11 arpeggio. These harmonic extensions we get from superimposing different pentatonic scales sound really cool, and work in all sorts of genres, although it is more of a jazz and fusion idea.

The lick in Example 98 is very reminiscent of how Shawn Lane does this sort of thing. Check out his celebrated album *Powers of Ten* to hear some of his amazing compositions and staggering technical ability. I would also recommend checking out the album *Centrifugal Funk* by the Mark Varney Project which includes Shawn Lane, Frank Gambale and Brett Garsed all on top form, playing their best fusion licks.

This particular album will showcase for you just how far you can push things with your legato, as Brett Garsed is pretty much the master in this field. Your sweeping, as obviously Frank Gambale is the master of this and, well pretty much everything is covered by Shawn as he was just a technical monster, capable of practically anything. Shawn would even blow the minds of most of the best guitarists, even being called by Paul Gilbert 'the most terrifying guy of all time'.

Example 98

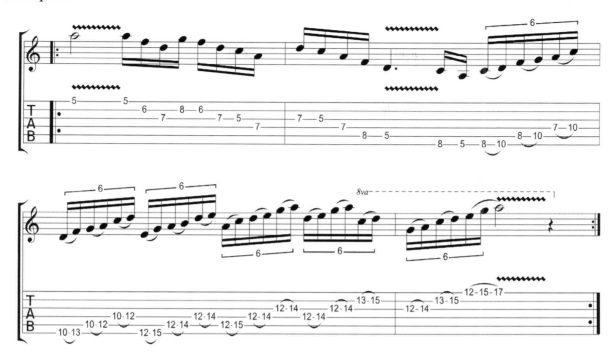

Example 99 is a lick for the jazzers among you. It's a II-V-I (2, 5, 1) lick in the key of C major. The II-V-I is the most common chord progression in jazz standards, and jazz soloists love to play over this progression. What it means, is that you are playing the second, fifth and first chord of whatever key you are playing in. In our case, in the key of C, it means we will be playing over a D minor 7, G dominant 7 and C major 7 chord progression.

The idea when soloing on this chord progression is to try to outline each chord by playing relevant notes from within each chord, or in other words hit the arpeggio which lives within the chord. When you get more advanced at playing over an II-V-I you can look at all sorts of superimpositions and substitutions but for now we will just use the standard approach.

In bar one of Example 99, we are playing over the D minor 7 chord, and outline this by hitting the notes of a D minor 11 arpeggio, a common extended jazz arpeggio. In bar two, we are playing the notes of a position two G7 arpeggio over the G7 chord, and finally finishing with a descending C major scale run on the C major 7 chord. Use alternate picking throughout this lick with the warmer sounding pickups like your neck pickup to get the tone, also try rolling off your tone knob a little and play with a clean channel on your amp.

If you like this idea and you are not familiar with jazz, I would recommend taking a listen to anything by guitarists such as Wes Montgomery, Joe Pass and George Benson, who are all amazing exponents of the II-V-I chord progression. Transcribing their licks will give you some great ideas on how to play over an II-V-I. Also, having an extremely good knowledge of all of your arpeggios all over the neck helps with this type of playing.

Example 99

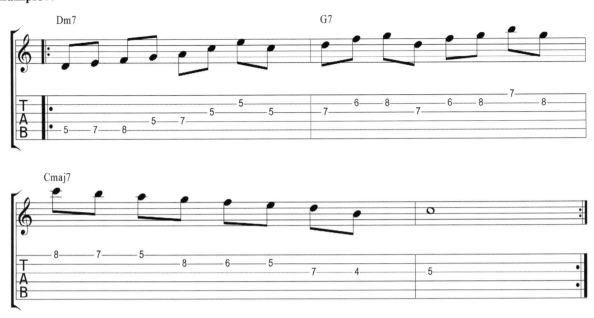

Example 100 is another II-V-I lick that incorporates chromatic passing tones to add harmonic interest to the lick. When playing long extended jazz solos, it can get a bit tedious hearing arpeggio after arpeggio. Chromaticism adds a bit of spice that can keep a listener interested. Chromatics are quite difficult to master, as if you meaninglessly meander around the neck playing chromatics, you start to sound like you don't know what you're doing.

However, when used correctly, it can sound really effective. Dave Brubeck's tune 'Take Five' is full of chromatics and people love the tune. The theme tune to the Pink Panther is also loaded with chromatics, so you can see that it certainly does work. To be honest, anybody familiar with the blues already uses chromatics, as the added flat five to the minor pentatonic scale is after all a chromatic note between the fourth and the fifth degree.

In Example 100, we begin playing over the Dm7 chord from the fifth to the ninth of D, and then we play a chromatic line that leads us from the ninth up to the eleventh of the chord. From here we play the fifth and root of D again before ending this bar on the b7 interval of D. This interval is also the eleventh in the next chord, G7, which we play a standard G7 arpeggio over. With the added eleventh at the beginning of G7 we outline a dominant 11 idea, which sounds very cool.

We end the G7 with a chromatic rundown that leads us nicely into a C major 7 arpeggio and finally a C major scale idea that finishes the lick. Once again use alternate picking throughout this lick to get the right feel, and also use the same tonal ideas that we mentioned in Example 99. To listen to a guitarist who adds a lot of chromatic lead lines in his II-V-I licks check out Pat Martino. I personally really like his album *Cream,* which features some of the scariest jazz soloing I've ever heard.

Example 100

In the next three examples, I want to show you how you can further break out of the boxes by using the full fretboard in one fluid lick. All the great guitarists are as capable at playing along the neck as they are across the neck. For you to become as good a player as you want to be, it's very important for you to also be able to unlock the fretboard in this manner.

When I say playing across the neck, what I mean is playing straight up and down box position scales in one area of the neck. Playing along the length of a single string is another way that we can play scales on the guitar. Being able to combine the ability to play across the neck and along the neck is how guitarists make the whole neck completely useable when soloing.

I always remember when I was at school, and I had not long gotten in to lead playing, I was pretty boxed in to minor pentatonic position one. I could play a few fast licks inside that shape and I could cross the scale pretty well, which ultimately led to my misguided idea that I was a good player. I took my guitar in to school for a band practice with a band I had recently joined, and there was a friend of mine who also played lead. We jammed for a bit, and I was immediately impressed by the fact that he could play along the length of the neck. It seemed as if he could use the whole guitar neck, and I was stuck in position one. It totally blew my mind and I realized then that I needed to be able to use more of the neck.

What I realized was that if I could play minor pentatonic ideas in this area and they sound great, then surely the same scale in another area of the neck will sound great too. It's just the same notes after all being played in different places. The really cool thing about the different shapes is that you have to play different licks in each one of them, as none of your licks from one position will move to another, due to the fact that the notes are ordered differently.

In Example 101, I've written a full fretboard lick using the A minor pentatonic scale, starting in position five in the lowest part of the neck, using legato and position shifts to get a nice gliding tone from one shape to the next. These kind of ideas are at home in any genre, and are used by all of the best guitarists. The lick has been demonstrated over a standard Am7 chord, so you can hear it in context.

Example 101

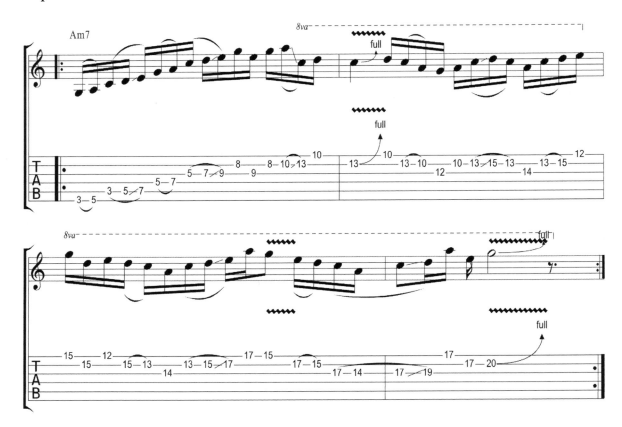

Example 102 is a similar idea to 101, starting in the low fifth position of A minor pentatonic, yet this time we are looking at picking all of the notes rather than using the legato technique. Feel free to use your preference of either alternate or economy picking. At this stage you should have had plenty of practice in playing each technique, and can now decide between which of the two you would choose when playing licks. Watch out for the tricky triplet rhythm that there is throughout this lick, and also make sure that you are using the correct fingerings by sliding neatly into each new position. If you get your fretting hand fingers in a muddle with this idea you will make it very hard for yourself.

Example 102

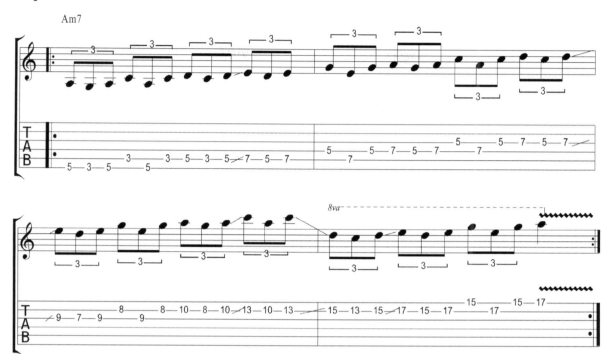

Example 103 is the last lick in this chapter, and shows you how you can build licks that move along just the higher notes in all five positions, rather than starting low and moving to the highest positions. You can of course move along the lower strings, the middle strings, whatever you choose. There are no rules really, you only need to follow the concept of, if it sounds good, it's good. Let your ears tell you whether you've played a good lick or sequence, and try not to be too governed by patterns and shapes.

I've written Example 103 using a mixture of hammers, pulls and slides for its execution, but please feel free to experiment with different picking approaches if you would prefer to play this way. Take extra care in the last bar of the lick, as we change from playing straight sixteenth notes to sixteenth note triplets, and the lick picks up a lot of speed towards the end.

Example 103

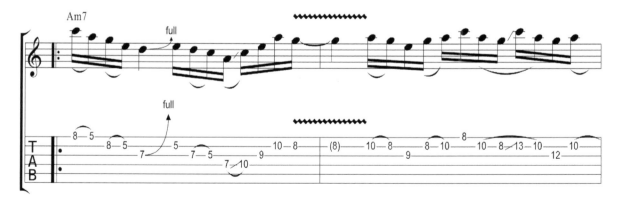

Example 103 concludes our licks chapter. In the previous twenty lick examples you should have found plenty of ideas to use as a springboard for creating your own licks in different styles. The licks presented will have given you a solid foundation for pentatonic phrasing, which is the staple scale used by all guitarists in all genres for soloing.

There are of course ideas that have shown you how to incorporate arpeggios and three notes per string playing, which we will now look to build upon further. In the next chapter we will look at how you can build longer, extended licks with more advanced concepts and maintain the level of technique that you will have gained from completing the examples in the book.

CHAPTER 8

Continued Development

As with Book One of this series, I thought it would be really useful to have a chapter at the end of the book that tells you what to do, once you have completed all of the examples and learnt the licks. It's all well and good being able to play a great tapping exercise, but it's a bit harder to know how to get that idea in to a song or solo you are working on. The continued development chapters in this series are here to help you progress after the book, and hopefully be able to make some great music with these ideas.

To make this chapter as useful as possible, I want to break it down in to two elements, firstly, the technical examples, and then secondly, the licks element to this book. What I would suggest first, is that if you are reading this part of the book and you have not yet worked all of the technical examples up to musical speeds, then go back and do so.

Use the building speed chapter to help you get all of the legato, picking, tapping and sweeping ideas up to a comfortable speed for playing at musical tempos, and then refer back to this point. Once you have worked all of the exercises up to a sufficient speed, the job of your continued development is to maintain that level of skill. Maintenance of your technique is one of the most important elements you can focus on in order to be able to play top level, professional music all of the time.

There is a saying that goes 'what you don't use, you lose' and this is so true. The really unfortunate thing is that it seems that we lose skills much quicker than we gain them, and this is why maintenance is so hugely important to being able to play at a top level. For the purpose of maintenance, you need to have some specific practice routines outlined. In Book One I outlined some example practice routines that would allow you to build your technique in all of the important areas. Now I will outline some perfect practice routines for maintenance in all of these areas, using the exercises in Book Two.

Again, like in Book One, I will outline some routines for fifteen minute, thirty minute, one hour and five hour practice sessions. This should cater for everybody's particular needs and their own particular schedules. After all, I do appreciate that not every guitar player has five full hours a day just to work on their chops, but absolutely everybody can find different points in a day where they can squeeze in a fifteen minute or half hour routine.

If you feel that you really can't find the time to practise, I would suggest asking yourself two questions. Firstly, how much do you really want to be a great guitar player? And secondly, what can you really cut back on to create time to play? The first question is obviously down to the individual, if you are not all that worried about being a great guitar player and you just want to play for fun, then that is absolutely fine. Slot in the time to practise when you feel like it, you will enjoy your guitar more this way.

If, however, you are answering this question with 'I want to be a pro' then really you should find the time no matter what! The answer to the second question is once again dependent on the individual's answer to question one. If you're not pushing to be a pro, and want to play for fun, of course you can do whatever it is you want to do in life and fit the guitar in around your other hobbies, work schedule etc.

If the answer to your second question is that you want to go pro, you need to find as much time as possible. Obviously you will need to work, eat, sleep, spend time with family etc., but what you really need to ask yourself about your time and where you can make your cutbacks, is do you really need to watch that TV programme? Do you really need to be out socializing with your friends as often as you do? Do you play a lot of PlayStation, X Box? How early do you get up in the morning? How much sleep do you really need? The list goes on and on.

So at this point you should have thought about how much practice you want to do. You have found fifteen minute, thirty minute, one hour and five hour slots all over your schedule so you know when you can fit some routines in. It's now the time to start having a look at how you can build these routines.

Fifteen minute routines

By their very nature, a fifteen minute routine is a short, high intensity blast routine in which you will play a few different exercises at your maxed-out speed. Playing your exercises in this way will most certainly keep them maintained at your highest level of playing possible. Please be aware though, that these routines can only be implemented once you have spent a lot of time working the exercises up to your highest speed.

To get the most versatility out of a fifteen minute blast routine, I would spend the first five minutes playing any of your favourite warm-up exercises from Book One. Perhaps it would be a good idea to choose some examples that require you to move around the neck, so you are covering a lot of ground. These sorts of exercises do tend to get the blood flowing a little better to your hands and fingers.

Another good idea you can try every now and then to mix it up, is spend five minutes playing through the linking the three notes per string exercise found in Chapter 1 of this book. Playing scales is a great way to warm up. Obviously you are not limited to playing this in the keys written, you can change keys as you see fit, thus learning the fretboard further. Once you have spent that first five minutes warming up, you will spend the next ten minutes playing ten different exercises at full tilt, for one minute each.

Make sure to take a few seconds rest here and there to shake out any tension you have created in your fretting hand, as we want to avoid injuries at all costs. When choosing exercises for the routine, I would suggest making each fifteen minute routine purely for one technique, so devise a fifteen minute legato, picking, sweeping and tapping routine.

I will now outline a fifteen minute routine for each technique that I have used. Each routine has not only gleaned good results in my playing, but as I love playing exercises on my guitar, I have actually found each routine rather enjoyable. Due to the short nature of these routines, I've also managed to squeeze them in to all parts of my day.

Sample fifteen minute Legato routine

Begin with five minutes warming up using any spider type exercise from Book One with hammers and pulls. Alternatively play through all three notes per string shapes using the linking shapes idea with hammers and pulls. Then play each of the following exercises from the Book Two legato chapter for one minute each in this order:

- Ex 12a/b (30 seconds each note grouping).
- Ex 13a/b (30 seconds each note grouping).
- Ex 14a/b (30 seconds each note grouping).
- Ex 15a/b (30 seconds each note grouping).
- Ex 17a/b/c (20 seconds each note grouping).
- Ex 18a/b/c (20 seconds each note grouping).
- Ex 19a/b/c (20 seconds each note grouping).
- Ex 4.
- Ex 2.
- Ex 3.

The routine outlined will hit quite a lot of areas covered in the chapter and I personally found it to be very useful. Feel free to swap in any of the other exercises from the chapter as you see fit to suit your own playing. Let's now take a look at a sample picking routine.

Sample fifteen minute Alternate Picking routine

Begin with five minutes warming up using any spider type exercise from Book One with alternate picking. Alternatively, play through all three notes per string shapes using the linking shapes idea with alternate picking. Then play each of the following exercises from the Book Two alternate picking chapter for one minute each in this order:

- Ex 23.
- Ex 24.
- Ex 27.
- Ex 28.
- Ex 29.
- Ex 30.
- Ex 31.
- Ex 32.
- Ex 33.
- Ex 34.

As you can see, this routine incorporates a lot of scale sequencing ideas. This is because I like to use a lot of these types of licks in my playing, however, feel free to swap some of these exercises for more of the arpeggio based examples if they suit you more. After all you should be looking to maintain the techniques which matter most in your music with these routines. Let's now take a look at a sample sweeping routine.

Sample fifteen minute Sweep routine

Begin with five minutes warming up using any warm-up exercise from Book One that can utilize the sweeping or economy picking technique. Alternatively play through all three notes per string shapes using the linking shapes idea with economy picking, or slowly play up and down some simple arpeggios shapes. Then play each of the following exercises from the Book Two sweep picking chapter for one minute each in this order:

- Ex 30.
- Ex 31.
- Ex 32.
- Ex 36.
- Ex 38.
- Ex 39.
- Ex 40.
- Ex 41.
- Ex 42.
- Ex 43.

The outlined routine gives a pretty good overview of all the three string sweeps we covered in this book, and is certainly an intense routine to play at full tilt. As always, if you feel there are some other exercises you would like to swap in to the routine, please make sure to do so. From time-to-time it won't hurt to swap the exercises in these routines anyway, to give your fingers new and fresh challenges. Let's conclude the fifteen minute routines with a sample tapping routine.

Sample fifteen minute Tapping routine

Begin with five minutes warming up using the same spider type exercise from Book One you used for your legato warm-up. Also, you can once again play through all three notes per string shapes using the linking shapes idea with hammers and pulls. Then play all ten examples from the tapping chapter in progressive order:

- Ex 44.
- Ex 45.
- Ex 46.
- Ex 47.
- Ex 48.
- Ex 49.
- Ex 50.

- Ex 51.
- Ex 52.
- Ex 53.

Due to the nature of the tapping chapter in this book being slightly shorter in terms of examples, there are only ten exercises for you to create your own routines. This isn't a problem at all, as the exercises are challenging in their own right and stretch you in many different ways. I have played them progressively in my routine, as I find they work nicely that way. You may wish to reorder them to suit your own style. There are no rules, just whatever works best for you.

The previous four routines outline the four chief technical areas for this kind of practice. Practising your bending and vibrato can be done in a similar manner, by taking the examples from that chapter and playing them over and again for one minute. However, I think it is far more beneficial to practise bending and vibrato by spending more time on one exercise.

For example, the vibrato exercise I outlined in the string bending and vibrato chapter, could easily be played solely for fifteen minutes. You could also spend a whole hour playing that one exercise. Expressive techniques need more time in developing feel, so please feel free to come up with lots of ways to practise the bending and vibrato ideas presented in the book for all sorts of time durations.

Now let's take a look at how I would personally develop thirty minute practice routines for the legato, alternate, sweep and tapping techniques. My own personal approach to this has always been to double up on everything I would do for a fifteen minute routine. For example, if I had planned to do a fifteen minute routine during a part of my working day, and a guitar student cancels a thirty minute lesson because they can't make it for some reason, I now find I have a thirty minute gap in my day with nothing to do.

Instantly I would fill that thirty minute gap in my day with practice time! After all, there is no point in sitting around doing nothing. So what I would do is take the pre-planned fifteen minute workout, and double it up so that I now have a good to go thirty minute routine. So you can see what I mean, I will outline a thirty minute sample legato routine.

Sample thirty minute Legato routine

Begin with ten minutes warming up using any spider type exercise from Book One with hammers and pulls. Alternatively play through all three notes per string shapes using the linking shapes idea with hammers and pulls. Then play each of the following exercises from the Book Two legato chapter for two minutes each in high intensity fashion. This means playing them at your maximum speed, stopping momentarily to shake out tension or take brief rests when experiencing pain. Play the exercises in this order for the following durations:

- Ex 12a/b (60 seconds each note grouping).
- Ex 13a/b (60 seconds each note grouping).
- Ex 14a/b (60 seconds each note grouping).
- Ex 15a/b (60 seconds each note grouping).

- Ex 17a/b/c (40 seconds each note grouping).
- Ex 18a/b/c (40 seconds each note grouping).
- Ex 19a/b/c (40 seconds each note grouping).
- Ex 4 – 2 minutes.
- Ex 2 – 2 minutes.
- Ex 3 – 2 minutes.

As you can see I have kept this routine exactly the same as the fifteen minute legato routine, except I have doubled each exercise's performance time in length. This way you get the same progressive order of technical work, but you are drilling the exercises in for longer. Half hour routines I personally found very useful in my late teens. In my late teens I was teaching guitar for a local music store, and pretty much all of my lessons were half hour in duration. What I would find is that gaps would regularly appear, due to the nature of lessons being in evenings or at weekends, people would often find other commitments would get in the way of their guitar lessons so every now and then couldn't make it.

I always figured that I would make use of this time by practising, and having a pre-prescribed routine that I could just follow worked perfectly, as when we are practising we often lose a bit of time thinking what to work on next. These half hour routines would always fill this time for me really well and moreover, I found half an hour to be a very productive amount of time to work on technique.

The next thing to look at is how we build these routines up to an hour in length. I've always believed that to get the very best out of any of the exercises I've come up with, your best bet is to try to play them for five minutes continuously. When drilling an exercise for five minutes I've always found that I made the best gains in terms of speed, fluidity, timing and tone. Making these exercises sound good is just as important as getting them to be fast, and practising each one for five minutes gives you the time to do so.

To build up one of these routines to an hour in length, I would still keep to ten exercises, so I would have a ten minute warm-up, and then fifty minutes of pure technical working. It's an extremely intense hour, playing these exercises at full tilt for five minutes each, but it certainly works for keeping your playing at the highest level. I will outline a one hour alternate picking routine, and with this principle being applied to the other technique areas you will be able to create one hour routines for each technique.

Sample one hour Alternate Picking routine

Begin with ten minutes warming up using any spider type exercise from Book One with alternate picking. Alternatively play through all three notes per string shapes using the linking shapes idea with alternate picking. Then play each of the following exercises from the Book Two alternate picking chapter for five minutes each. Play them in high intensity fashion, at your full speed, stopping only when experiencing pain or fatigue. Shake the tension out, rest for around ten seconds or until the pain subsides and play that exercise again until the five minutes is up. Again play the exercises progressively in the following order:

- Ex 23.
- Ex 24.

- Ex 27.
- Ex 28.
- Ex 29.
- Ex 30.
- Ex 31.
- Ex 32.
- Ex 33.
- Ex 34.

Once again, I've used the same exercises as the fifteen minute routine, in the same order, as this is a routine that really benefitted me. I also like keeping my routines the same as it's easy to scale up or scale down the length of time I want to practise for, depending on how my schedule is looking. By all means though be creative with these routines and come up with something that works for you.

You may have particular weaknesses in your playing and want to work on these areas for longer. This may mean that you may want to spend ten minutes on certain exercises. When you're in this maintenance phase it's entirely up to you what you work on. Let's not forget, if you have worked up an exercise to a really good speed, yet you feel it sounds a little sloppy, you can slow it back down and gradually work your way up the metronome again, making sure that as you go up in tempo your licks are sounding clean and fluid.

You can also incorporate the rhythmic displacement ideas from the developing speed chapter to make your licks better. This means that in a one hour routine you could look at playing just one exercise, constantly rotating the note on the downbeat to make the lick sound absolutely perfect. This seems like a lot of work, but having this level of technical command on your instrument can only be a good thing. Not only will it mean that you are capable of learning new things faster, and playing much more music in a cleaner, more capable way, but it will give you the confidence to know that under the pressures of live performance, recording, auditions etc., that you will be able to perform at a high level.

We have looked at how to build these routines up to a point where you have enough ideas to get a one hour routine, let's now look at a full five hour practice routine that will stretch the players among you that want to go all out and play guitar as much as possible. A five hour practice routine purely for technique is not for the faint-hearted. However, if you want to be as good as you can possibly be, playing guitar for hours every day is what it takes.

Many of the best guitarists out there will say that they played guitar fourteen hours a day when they were young, because life permitted them to do so and that was all they wanted to do. Personally, I have never played for that long in one day just purely practising. I have played guitar for a full eight hours, and have more frequently racked up a seven hour day (equivalent to a working day) of practising the guitar.

When practising a full five hours purely on technique, I would usually divide up my time like this: thirty minutes warming up. One hour each for the four chief technique areas, i.e. legato, alternate picking, sweeping and tapping. And a final thirty minutes of practising improvisation, including licks, work on bending and vibrato.

It would be very fair to say that the final thirty minutes is far too short to fully practise improvisation and expressive techniques. I completely agree that it's not enough time to invest in these areas if this is the way you practise all the time, but this is just one routine that I may use. The focus of this routine is purely to get better on technique. If I'm really concerned with improvising, I might make a whole five hour afternoon all about improvisation.

The thing with practising improvisation is that you are always working on your different technique areas anyway, and it certainly is a great way to practise. My thought process to the routines I used in the beginning was that I wanted to be able to play amazing solos, so first I would need the technique, then once I had it, the technique would be maintained by the high level of the 'playing' that I was doing.

I'm pretty sure that all of the great guitarists I have mentioned throughout these two books no longer spend all of their time practising their 'chops' so to speak. It is obvious though that once upon a time they did, and now their amazing technique is maintained by the fact that they are out there playing extremely difficult music, night after night. Let's now take a look at a sample five hour practice routine that I would use with the exercises in this book, to give me a general rounded technique.

Sample five hour technique practice routine

Warm-up

Begin with thirty minutes warming up using any exercises you want from Book One's warm-up chapter. Also playing up and down three notes per string scales is advised. Use the linking the scales idea and also you may want to play each shape in every position up to the twelfth fret and back, this would really get you nicely warmed up for the session that follows.

Legato hour

Choose ten to twelve exercises from the legato chapter and divide the hour evenly between each exercise. You can play them in any order you wish. I would advise playing cycled lick type exercises before playing any sequences. The cycled licks will serve to really prepare your fretting hand for the string crosses you will face when playing a run. Even if the runs are pentatonic, in this book they are still pretty demanding. I have chosen the same ten exercises as the one hour routine we looked at previously but I would now do something like this:

- Ex 12a/b (3 minutes each note grouping).
- Ex 13a/b (3 minutes each note grouping).
- Ex 14a/b (3 minutes each note grouping).
- Ex 15a/b (3 minutes each note grouping).
- Ex 17a/b/c (2 minutes each note grouping)
- Ex 18a/b/c (2 minutes each note grouping).
- Ex 19a/b/c (2 minutes each note grouping).

- Ex 4 – 6 minutes.
- Ex 2 – 6 minutes.
- Ex 3 – 6 minutes.

Alternate Picking hour

Straight after the legato hour I would move straight into an hour of alternate picking. I always ordered my routines in order of importance that I felt I would use them in my own improvisation, and in sensible mechanical orders. Once my fretting hand was completely warm from all of the legato exercises, I would then seek to sync up my two hands using alternate picking. Only then would I move on to sweeps to get my mind thinking about arpeggios before finishing with tapping. Once again, when alternate picking, pick ten to twelve exercises and play them in any order you wish. For this routine I have chosen twelve picking exercises that I would play for five minutes each. I would probably do something like this:

- Ex 23.
- Ex 24.
- Ex 25.
- Ex 26.
- Ex 27.
- Ex 28.
- Ex 29.
- Ex 30.
- Ex 31.
- Ex 32.
- Ex 33.
- Ex 34.

As you can see, I've worked progressively through the examples starting at Example 23 and finishing at 34. I feel that these examples give me a nicely rounded workout that fits neatly into the hour, and I like to work progressively. You may wish to start with the scalar example and then move to the arpeggios. Once again, the choice is yours. Next up, we have an hour of sweeping.

Sweep Picking hour

Now that my two hands would be nicely synced and warm, I would begin looking at sweeping. With sweeping we would now be moving away from scalar territory and beginning arpeggios. I would begin a sweeping routine by just playing singular arpeggios and then moving into runs that move along the neck. For this particular routine I've chosen twelve exercises and would play each for five minutes. I would start slowly for the first two minutes of each new exercise, as sweeping is so wildly different to the previous techniques. Then I would blast the last three minutes of each exercise. The exercises I have selected for the routine go like this:

- Ex 30.
- Ex 31.
- Ex 32.
- Ex 36.
- Ex 33.
- Ex 34.
- Ex 35.
- Ex 37.
- Ex 38.
- Ex 39.
- Ex 40.
- Ex 42.

I've ordered the sweeping exercises in a manner that allows individual arpeggios to be practised before putting those shapes together to create runs. It makes a lot of sense to practise individual parts of a run before trying the whole thing, not only with sweeping but with all large licks. Paul Gilbert likes to break his licks up into tiny parts when practising them, before sticking it all together to create the full lick. If it works for Paul, who is obviously a technical monster, then it will be good enough for you too.

The last four examples I have chosen to use in this routine are all extended runs, but feel free to practise little parts of them for maybe a minute or so each before running the full lick for a few minutes. At the end of the day, as long as you have managed the full hour and practised your licks in high intensity fashion, you've certainly had a good workout for your sweeping. Let's now move on to an hour of tapping.

Tapping hour

By this stage of the routine, we've thoroughly warmed up, we've synced up both hands and now have familiarized our ears with the sound of scales and arpeggios. This means we are now ready to take on an hour of tapping. Once again due to the nature that this technique is so different to sweeping, I would begin slowly, building up the speed throughout each exercise. As there are ten examples in the tapping chapter, I would aim to play each example for six minutes, divided into two minutes at a slow tempo, two minutes at a medium tempo and two minutes in all out high intensity fashion. This way you get the most rounded workout possible as you are practising all tempos and all of the exercises in the chapter.

With the tapping routine, you could also choose just six of the exercises and play them for ten minutes each. I've often had good results when stepping up the level of practice from five or six minutes up to ten minutes. Be aware though that when practising an exercise for ten minutes it is very hard to maintain high intensity fashion throughout. It would be worth practising for around five minutes at a medium tempo and then five minutes in high intensity. This way your mind and fingers will have complete command of the lick from the first five minutes drilling it in. This will then allow your high intensity burst to be easier. If I were aiming to choose six examples from the chapter to practise in this way, I would probably do something like this:

- Ex 44.
- Ex 45.
- Ex 46.
- Ex 51.
- Ex 52.
- Ex 53.

These six examples would give you a nicely rounded overview of the technique in the chapter, and as they are each pretty demanding in different ways, you should find it an entertaining routine to follow as well as being highly useful. Either approach to the tapping routine outlined would be an excellent use of your hour. As always, you can by all means create your own routine that suits your own needs. Once you've finished the tapping hour, we will finish this five hour session with thirty minutes of improvisation, and an added focus to bending and vibrato.

Improvisation and expressive techniques

I would always finish every session with at least half an hour of jamming or playing some tunes. With the amount of time we have spent on all the other areas, we would have thirty minutes left over to finish our session. I personally would like to use this time to practise my improvisation. At the same time when improvising, you can make sure to practise good vibrato and string bending. Jamming along to music is really important, as not only is it very fun (and playing the guitar should always be fun) but it's the best way to learn all the things about music that a technical exercise can't teach you. You can practise your feel, your tone, when to add these awesome licks you have learned and more importantly, when not to.

Practising this element of your playing requires far more attention than just thirty minutes at the end of a long technical workout. I'm not suggesting at all that this is the only way you practise. In fact, I think it's a brilliant idea to mix it all up as much as possible to make you a more rounded musician. I'm merely stating that in the case of a technical workout it does help to finish with thirty minutes jamming.

This nice end to the routine allows you to use the technique you have been practising and see how it works in musical context. I would strongly urge that you also put a lot of focus into string bending and vibrato. Also be conscious of your tone. Try to improve it. Play fast, shallow, wide, slow vibrato. Play vibrato on all your different fingers and on different strings. The more rounded and polished you can make this element of your playing the better.

When jamming and practising playing in this final thirty minutes, you should always be playing along to some sort of backing track. You will want this part of your routine to sound as musical as possible, so having the drums, some harmony and a good bass line to play with are all really important factors. Another great practice tool is a loop pedal, as with one of these you can loop up a chord progression, getting in some practice for your rhythm chops, and then solo over the top.

Once you've had your thirty minutes of jam time at the end, you will have completed a pretty monster routine for technical workouts. Let's recap the ideas we have discussed so that you can keep fresh in your mind exactly how to perform such a lengthy and intense practice session.

Five hour practice session at a glance

- ✓ Thirty minutes warm-up time.
- ✓ One hour of legato exercises.
- ✓ One hour of alternate picking exercises.
- ✓ One hour of sweep picking exercises.
- ✓ One hour of tapping exercises.
- ✓ Thirty minutes of improvisation and expressive technique.

At this point you should have lots of ideas on how best to create your own practice routines, so that you can completely master and maintain the level of technique that can be achieved from reading **High Intensity Guitar Technique Book Two**. At the beginning of the chapter, I mentioned breaking your continued development down into two concepts.

The first being the technique, which I think we have covered quite comprehensively by now. The second is the licks, and how you are going to get your newfound technique into your music. Let's start thinking about how we can begin making all this awesome new technique work for us, and achieve the ultimate goal, which is to make better and more interesting music.

The first thing you need to do is make the licks in chapter seven become your own. You can only really use the licks once they have become second nature, and they will sound their most musical when they just come out in your playing, rather than if you're just trying to squeeze them in. Once you have each lick mastered, you must start trying to play these licks as a part of your own improvised solos.

Once you are familiar with the licks and can use them in a way you feel you are happy with, what you need to do next is use the licks as a stepping stone to creating your very own ideas. Keeping with the pentatonic theme for a moment, what I would suggest is that you create your own lick bank of around ten licks you really like, in every one of the five positions. This will obviously give you fifty licks to draw upon when soloing.

Many of my students have said to me that they find it very hard to create licks. It's understandably so, because when you don't know where to start with any subject it's always so hard to get going. What I want to share with you is the same nuggets of inspiration I've given to my students. Start by thinking about what the point is you want to get across. Do you want to play something fast or slow? Do you want something with big bends, or slides? Will this lick be smooth and legato, or aggressive and picked? What notes do you want to hit, in terms of interval?

When you can answer questions like this you can already be thinking about the exact notes you want to play, in what order, and which technique you are going to use to be able to play them. The next problem is rhythm. Students often know which notes they want to play, and they can tell me which technique they want to use to execute the lick. The problem they have is they don't know **how** to play the lick, and by this they mean they don't know how rhythmically to play it.

My advice to my students struggling with this, is for them to think about what the lick is trying to say. The word 'say', is the key word here, as when we are playing music, we are trying to express ourselves in a musical way, and make musical statements. So if we are trying to say something with the guitar, is it a feasible idea that we can use our speech to give us cool rhythms to use for playing our licks with? I think so.

When my students struggle with a rhythm for a lick, I always say something to the student, then we capture that rhythm, put the notes to it and voila. I'm not going to suggest that this is the only answer to creating good rhythms for licks, but it is a starting point. If I had a pound for every time I heard the phrase 'he makes the guitar talk' when I was growing up as a student of the guitar, I would be a rich man.

So if we are obsessed with great guitarists who can make the guitar talk, then surely looking to our speech for rhythms isn't such a bad idea. Let's try this idea out for size. If I take the common phrase 'Hey, how are you today' this phrase has six syllables. If I say that phrase out loud four different ways and notate the rhythms, it could go something like this:

If I were to now add some notes from the minor pentatonic scale into these rhythms, I could end up with four licks that sound like Example 104.

Example 104

Surprisingly enough, the individual licks sound relatively musical don't they? And when you put them all together you have a scalar passage that sounds like a decent bit of lead guitar playing. Now don't get me wrong, I'm not saying that this method is the answer to writing great guitar licks, it's just one way you could try. There are rhythms all around us all of the time, so feel free to steal from Mother Nature whenever possible.

Guthrie Govan did so for his song 'Fives' for which he copied a couple of birds singing. Many musicians have been inspired by the sound of water falling, in either rain or waterfalls. Some musicians have been inspired by the sound of train wheels or by car engines and an odd rhythmic pulse. Inspiration is everywhere if you just keep your ears open.

I have talked a lot throughout these books about the importance of using your ears and transcribing great guitarists. For sure there is no better way to learn a whole bunch of awesome blues licks, than listening to your favourite blues guitarist and working out exactly how he or she plays the way they do. By this same token you may be inspired by the sound of some great music that is not played on the guitar.

In the sweep picking chapter of this book I mentioned my love for Irish music, and especially fiddle and flute ideas. Transcribing these instruments has given me some great ways to stretch my legato technique and allowed me to find sounds I never would have thought of if I just listened to the guitar. Always think creatively and with an open mind about how you can improve your music and you will find that the ways you can stretch your playing are pretty limitless.

You can expand your lick bank by incorporating more of the three notes per string ideas we have discussed in this book. In the licks chapter I kept everything relatively boxed in to pentatonic world, as for the guitar player this is what you will find yourself playing for most of your solos, especially if you are in a covers band and playing famous guitar solos.

You can quite easily break away from this pentatonic framework by incorporating lots more three notes per string ideas into your playing. In order to do this, I would first recommend learning the sound of each mode that can be created by playing the three notes per string shapes I outlined over different chords. For example, we have the C major scale written all over the whole neck in three notes per string form. The C major scale contains the notes C, D, E, F, G, A and B. When we play these notes over a C major or C major 7 chord, the notes all sound like the C major scale. Yet if we play these same notes over a D minor 7 chord, we get the sound of the D Dorian mode, which is a particularly nice sounding minor scale.

All major scales have seven different modes, being Ionian (major scale itself), Dorian, Phrygian, Lydian, Mixolydian, Aeolian (natural minor scale, the relative minor of the major scale) and Locrian. These seven different modes all present themselves when we play the different chords that live within a key. When we outline the chords that live in one key, we call that harmonizing the scale. If I harmonize the C major scale we get the following chords:

Cmaj7, Dm7, Em7, Fmaj7, G7, Am7, Bm7b5.

When we have the C major 7 chord as our backing chord and play the three notes per string shapes for C major, we are outlining the C Ionian mode (otherwise known as the C major scale). If we change the chord to Dm7, we now hear D Dorian. For Em7 we would hear E Phrygian, Fmaj7 gives us F Lydian, G7 Gives us G Mixolydian, Am7 gives us A Aeolian and Bm7b5 gives us B Locrian.

I would suggest playing the scale shapes over all of the chords so you can begin to hear each individual mode. The theory behind modes is not quite as important as being able to hear them. The formulas in terms of which chord and mode fit together, transposes itself into all of the other keys too. So for example, if you encounter a Bm7 chord, this chord can be interpreted as either a B Dorian or a B Aeolian chord, so you can solo on it using these approaches.

To get a further grip of the theory behind the modes, I would recommend taking a look at Mark Levine's rather exceptional *The Jazz Theory Book*, which covers practically every theoretical concept in great detail and explains fully the theory behind modes. Once you have the sound of the modes of C major in your inner ear, you can begin creating lots of licks within these three notes per string shapes by using similar methods to that of our pentatonic style licks.

If you revisit the legato chapter and the alternate picking chapter of this book, you will find there are lots of different three notes per string examples. How many of the cycled exercises or sequenced runs can become great licks when you add an awesome string bending exit to them? Just an idea…

At this point you should be filled with lots of ideas on how to continue your development with your technical exploits. You will now have lots of new ideas about how to create practice routines that will keep your playing fresh and at a high level, as long as you are prepared to put in the effort required. Also you have now learned several ways that you can incorporate your newfound technique into your playing.

When you have successfully polished your technique up, you have lots of licks under your belt and you are bursting full of fresh music that you want to come flooding out of your guitar, head on over to the next section of the book where you will find some jam tracks for you to practise soloing over.

CHAPTER 9

Jam Tracks

In this chapter, we will be taking a look at the included backing tracks that are on the accompanying download for this book. The backing tracks that accompany this book are an invaluable resource for practising your new-found technique in a musical way. If you have come through both Book One and Two of this series so far, you will have learned lots of new techniques and cool licks, and I thought it would be fun to give you some ideas on how to use them in a proper musical context.

I have composed seven different backing tracks, all in different styles so that you can get a feel for how to perform in different genres. You will also see how your note choice will need to change in different genres, even though the technique will be the same. I've composed two blues tracks, a rock track, a funk track, a fusion track, a jazz track and finally a metal track. Using your technique in these different genres will be really useful to you in making you a rounded, polished and professional guitarist.

Track 1

Our first jam track is Example 105, and is a minor blues progression in the style of B.B. King's famous song 'The Thrill is Gone'. This track will give you the perfect platform for practising your minor pentatonic ideas. Pay close attention to your string bending and vibrato when playing on this track, as a minor blues is usually a very emotional style of music that carries a lot of passion and soul. I personally feel that emphasizing your pentatonic legato chops on this track will give you the best tone, but as always, music is a subjective thing, so whatever feels right, go for it.

I've written the track in the key of A minor, and the progression follows a standard minor blues which I will outline in Example 105. This means for soloing you can use the A minor pentatonic scale as a safe bet. You can also add in certain intervals like the ninth (B) to add a sophisticated quality to your licks. You can use the A natural minor scale sparingly on this chord progression too, but try not to get too 'shreddy' with your three notes per string shapes here, we can save that for later.

On the Track 1 audio, you will find that there is one version of the track where I have played a demo solo, so you can get an idea of how to play on the track, and then there is the full backing track which you can jam on. The chord progression for this track is outlined in Example 105 so you know what chords you are playing on.

Example 105

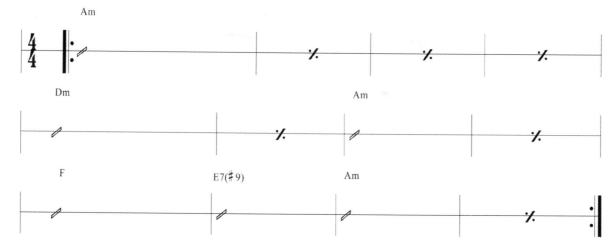

Track 2

Our second jam track is another blues, but this time it's a dominant blues instead of a minor blues. In a dominant blues, we follow the same one, four, five chord progression as a normal blues, except that all of the chords are now dominant 7 chords. This means that when soloing on them, we have a few more options than our straight minor pentatonic scale.

When playing over this chord progression you can use the standard A minor pentatonic over the whole progression, which will work perfectly. Or you can aim to hit the tones of each chord, by playing the relative arpeggios that fit over the chord. For example, on the A7 chord, the relevant arpeggio is an A dominant 7 arpeggio. To play this arpeggio, you need to play an A major arpeggio with an added seventh interval.

If you revisit the arpeggio shapes from Book One of this series, you will find the major arpeggio shapes written in the key of C. To add a flat seven interval to them, you need to add in a note that is a tone below each root note, and then you will have the dominant 7 arpeggios. Then if you transpose those shapes to fit over an A7, D7 and E7 chord, you can use these arpeggios to jam over the track.

The other thing you may wish to do when playing over this track is to play the full Mixolydian mode for each chord. This would mean transposing your major scale shapes, in either three notes per string or box positions, whichever you prefer, to fit over these chords. The easiest way to do this is to learn which three major scales the chords in this blues belong to.

A7 is the fifth chord in the key of D major. So if you play the D major scale on this chord you will get the sound of the A Mixolydian mode. The D7 chord is the fifth chord in the key of G, so if you transpose your major scales to the key of G for this one you will hear D Mixolydian. Finally, if you play the A major scale on the E7 chord, this will give you E Mixolydian.

You could also try mixing major and minor pentatonic ideas over these chords, and for any of you players reading this that have a more advanced concept of harmony and theory, you can try transposing all sorts of different arpeggios and chords in here to get cool sounds. Again this is a subjective field, so play whatever feels right, and whatever sounds good to you.

In terms of what technique to practise on this track, this one is a little less restraining than our previous blues track. You can use any techniques you like on this one and don't be afraid to play fast, as this is a much flashier style of blues playing. Take a listen to Guthrie Govan's mind-blowing blues playing to hear how far you can push this sort of thing. In Example 106 I have outlined the chord progression, which has the Hendrix E7#9 chord added into the turnaround to give us a nice jazzy edge to this blues. I have once again given you a demo solo and then the full backing track in the Track 2 audio.

Example 106

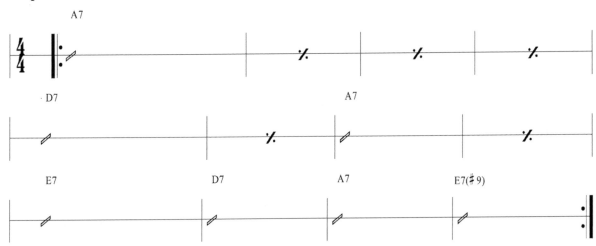

Track 3

Our third jam track is one for the rockers among you. I've composed this track with chords that belong to the A Aeolian mode (natural minor scale). This means the three notes per string shapes for that scale that you've learned earlier in the book will be perfect for drawing upon when soloing on the track. You can also use your good old faithful minor pentatonic scale on this one. Being a rock track, this one lends itself to really going for it with your technique. You can practise all of your sweeping, tapping, legato and picking chops all over this one. Pay close attention to your bending and vibrato too on this track. Make sure it's nice and wide and stylistically right for the rock genre. Track 3 can be found in the audio accompaniment where you will find a demo solo from me and the full backing track.

Track 4

Our fourth jam track is a funk piece that has been composed around two different static D minor 7 vamps. In modern jazz/funk fusion, it is very common to find a long extended vamp on one chord in solo sections. This track provides you the perfect platform for practising your Dorian modal chops in the key of D minor. D Dorian is the second mode of C major, so you will not need to transpose any shapes around the neck, the shapes you already know will give you the sound of the D Dorian mode. When playing over a static minor 7 chord the Dorian mode is quite often the best choice of scale for improvisers, so this will give you a great opportunity to hone your skills with this scale. As for the technique, again, anything goes.

This track has been composed in the style of fusion players such as Greg Howe, who is a technical monster. So feel free to really go for it on this one, always making sure you are playing musically. Although the track is viewed as static Dm7, on the recording I've played chords that add in the natural sixth of the Dorian mode, to hammer home the flavour of the mode. I've also used some extended minor 9 and minor 11 sounds here and there. The track can be found on the audio, again with a demo solo from me and the backing track. I've outlined the two basic rhythm parts that are on the track in Example 108, labelled as vamp A and vamp B. This will give you a rough idea of what's being played on the track, and show you how to create vamps such as this yourself by using different voicings of one chord.

Example 108

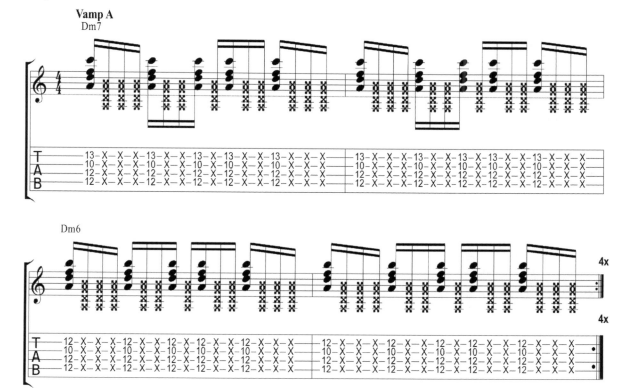

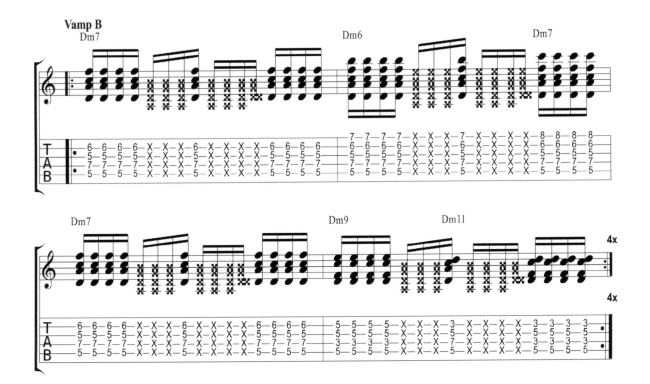

Track 5

Our fifth jam track is a fusion piece that combines elements of jazz, funk and rock. The track is focussed on two different dominant 7 riff type vamps that are completely unrelated in key. This means that you will need to treat each vamp as an individual, rather than using a one scale fits all approach.

Being a dominant vamp, the Mixolydian mode is the one to go for. The first vamp is based on G7, which means we need to use the G Mixolydian mode. To do this you can use any of the C major scale shapes found in these books, as the C major scale contains all of the same notes as G Mixolydian. The second vamp is the exact same pattern of notes but being played a minor third higher, from Bb. This means we need to use the Bb Mixolydian mode. To do this you can move any soloing idea you play on the G7 up three frets and it will work on Bb7.

Alternatively, you could find the correct Bb Mixolydian shape that lives in the same fretboard territory as the G Mixolydian shape you are soloing in. This will give you the smoothest transition of notes in terms of sound. Bb Mixolydian comes from the parent key of Eb major, so use Eb major scales as a reference for finding the Bb Mixolydian notes.

In terms of technique applicable to this track, well, anything goes. This sort of jazz/rock/funk fusion is very popular among guitar virtuosos, who aren't afraid of using any amount of technique, so again you can really go for it on this one. Try not to get too lost in your soloing though and forget about the changes; make sure you are always playing something that sounds good, not just something fast.

In Example 109 I have outlined the backing track riffs for each dominant vamp. You will see that the riff draws heavily upon notes from the Mixolydian mode, making sure to point you in that soloing direction.

Example 109

Track 6

Our sixth jam track is a jazz track based on standards like 'Autumn Leaves'. The most important chord progression in jazz is the II-V-I, and in this track you have the perfect platform for practicing your II-V-I licks over both a major and a minor II-V-I. The chord progression is composed of a II-V-I in C major and a II-V-I in A minor. This means the chords follow the progression shown in Example 110.

Example 110

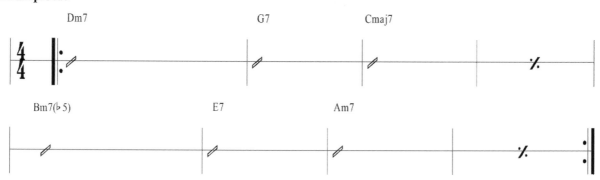

An II-V-I chord progression is always made up of a second, fifth and first chord of any key. This is how we arrive at the chord progression in Example 110, as we have used the chord progression in both C major and A minor. The great thing about C major and A minor, is that they are relative major and minor keys. This means any soloing idea that you will use on a C major chord progression works perfectly well on the A minor progression.

When playing over this track you can use solely the C major and A minor pentatonic scales we have looked at in the book, however, this isn't the way that most jazzers tend to play. Jazz guitarists create II-V-I licks like the ones we saw in our licks chapter. Use this track for trying to come up with your own II-V-I ideas. From a technical perspective, jazzers tend to pick most of their notes, as the tone for this style of music is quite unforgiving for the legato technique.

Essentially you want a warm clean tone from your amp, neck pickup selected on the guitar with the tone control rolled down. This way you get a really smooth clean tone, which is great for playing alternate or economy picked lines, but not so great when using lots of hammer-ons and pull-offs. Also steer clear of wide bends and vibrato; jazzers more often use a classical style vibrato that comes from sliding the finger back and forth inside a fret. Too much string bending and wide vibrato doesn't fit the sophisticated sound of the jazz genre. As always, take a listen to my demo solo and then jam on the full-length track.

Track 7

Our seventh track is the final track for this chapter, and is a metal style track composed in the style of acts such as Metallica and Megadeth. This one draws heavily upon the E Phrygian mode, which is the third mode in the key of C major. Once again, this means that as far as soloing on the track is concerned, using your three notes per string C major scales will be a safe bet, as when these are played over an E minor backing, they give you the sound of the Phrygian mode. You will also find that moving your pentatonic scale to the key of E minor will give you some suitably Metallica-esque results.

I've saved this track till last because in terms of technique, this one really is an anything goes kind of affair. Feel free to push the boundaries as far as you can go with this one, as the metal style really lends itself to outlandish style face-melting lead guitar. Any amount of sweeping, tapping, long flowing legato lines or aggressive alternate picked licks will sound great on this track so feel free to do what you please. I've once again added a demo solo you can get an idea of different things you can try on the track. You will also find the full backing track on the audio accompaniment, so what are you waiting for? Let rip!

In this chapter you have looked at playing over blues, rock, funk, fusion, jazz and metal backings, which are genres that are all quite varied in the way we play over them. From studying the technique thoroughly in this book, you will be able to create lots of awesome new licks in these styles. The more you practise playing over the tracks, you will greatly expand your improvisational potential in these different genres too, helping to make you a more cutting edge guitarist.

Afterword

Having reached the end of this book, you've come through quite a demanding text that will hopefully have stretched your ability, taking you from a decent guitar player to a highly polished, professional sounding musician. You will now have a great technical facility in many areas of playing the guitar; you will also have a better understanding of how guitar playing legends have attained such high levels with their instrument. Like them, you will now be able to create licks and solos of your own at a high level.

Always bear in mind that the music you are trying to create with your newfound technique is absolutely the most important thing. Always be mindful of the notes you are playing, and never try to just add in a flash lick or play notes for the sake of it. Your audiences will find your playing much more impressive if you put your coolest licks in at the right times. As guitarists, we are always trying to impress, and more often than not we are very concerned with what everyone else will think of our playing. This is one reason why so many players tend to 'overplay'. However, it is overplaying that makes you sound less of a musician, and more of a noodling guitarist.

Obviously you will want to be using all the techniques you have looked at in this book, but make sure you're not trying to impress people with a 'look at me' kind of feel. Just make sure that it is your musicality that is driving your songs, and now your professional level technique will allow you to play lots of varied music. The short of this theme, is to just play what is in your heart. Play the music that you love, and let your technique allow you to play the sounds in your head. This way you will create the most beautiful music you can make, and hopefully others will want to listen to you play.

For those of you reading this that are still curious about how far you can push the limits of guitar technique, you may be interested to check out the third instalment of this series which will take you from professional levels all the way through to virtuoso levels of technique. If you want to push your guitar playing skills to the absolute limit, and reach the super high standards of the best guitarists that have ever lived, the third book in this series, simply called **High Intensity Guitar Technique Book 3: Virtuoso Techniques** shows you how to reach an ultra level of guitar ability.

If you're looking for more help than a book can offer, membership to my all-in-one learning platform Cutting Edge Guitar offers advanced online courses, lesson packs, and various degrees of access to get help, support and feedback from me. You can find out more here **www.cuttingedge.guitars**

It's been my pleasure sharing my passion for guitar with you in this book, and I wish you all the best with your musical endeavours.

ABOUT THE AUTHOR

Anthony George started playing the guitar at 13 years old and by the time he was 17, was already teaching his first students. Aged 20, Anthony became a graduate of London's prestigious Guitar Institute, part of the Institute Of Contemporary Music Performance. Since 2012 Anthony has been the director of the guitar tuition company, Cutting Edge Guitar ltd, which originally operated in schools and from its own studio in Northampton, teaching in excess of 100 students per week. Today, Cutting Edge Guitar has become an all-in-one online learning platform that delivers the most detailed and structured advancing guitar player courses, lesson packs and books, all designed to rapidly improve your guitar skills.

To find out more about Anthony and Cutting Edge Guitar visit **www.cuttingedge.guitars**

Made in United States
Troutdale, OR
07/23/2023